Misplac

God

(and finding
Him again)

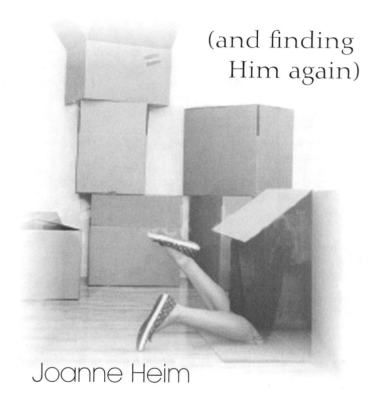

Joanne Heim

Kregel
Publications

Printed in the United States of America
09 10 11 12 13 / 5 4 3 2 1

For Janna, my friend,
and for Kathy, my new sister

Contents

Acknowledgments

Have you heard the saying, "It takes a village to raise a child"? Well, it takes a village to make a book as well. Writing a book is hard work, and I couldn't do it without the help of so many. So let me say thank you . . .

To my incredible husband, Toben, who encourages me to be the woman God created me to be.

To my sweet children, Audrey and Emma, who teach me so much about what it means to have a childlike faith.

To my parents, Chuck and Kay Friedenstein, who are wonderful parents and role models.

To my friends—you know who you are!—who pray for me, encourage me, and make my life so rich.

To the women who read my blog, pray faithfully for me, and share so much of their lives with me. Your quick responses when I've asked for your help and input have been so amazing. It's such a privilege to know you—I long for heaven when we can sit face to face.

To my agent, Bill Jensen, who is my friend.

And most of all, to my Abba, who loves me and has delivered me. You are my joy and I love you.

Have You Misplaced God?

Somehow I misplaced God. In the midst of growing up and getting married, starting a career and then a family, I lost track of him. He wasn't out of the picture completely—I knew he was around . . . somewhere . . . but I just couldn't put my hand on him at a given moment.

It's not as though I misplaced him on purpose. I went to church, was part of a small group, and I didn't doubt his existence. I knew I'd see him on Sunday morning at church, at Bible study on Thursday, and perhaps at night when I tucked my kids into bed. He was still part of my life, but somewhere on the fringe. He wasn't the center of my day-to-day life—driving around, going to work, hanging out with friends, and spending time with family. I wanted him to be central, but I didn't quite know how to make that happen.

I went through phases of having quiet times, but it never lasted long. Quiet time was a good place to start, but it didn't feel like enough. Spending time with God each morning started something off right, but it quickly stalled as the day got underway and filled with so many other things. I wanted more.

It happens to many of us. We sit in church on Sunday mornings and long to soak in his presence, to make this week different, to "practice the presence of God" as Brother Lawrence said so well. We leave church knowing God is real, and we want to take that certainty with us throughout the week.

We want to spend time with him each day, to grow in relationship together. But making prayer a daily commitment or reading the Bible or finishing this week's Bible study homework somehow gets pushed lower and lower on our list of priorities.

I have a lot of lists: the list of things to pick up at the grocery store, the list of chores to do, the list of errands to run. It's often not until the end of the day that I remember I wanted to make today different—to spend quality time with God. *I blew it again*, I think, and resolve to make tomorrow better.

Can you relate? But when tomorrow comes and life pushes in from all directions, we find ourselves once again hoping for a realness with God that we can't seem to find.

The desire is there and it's real. Why is it so easy to misplace it, so difficult to follow through? We want more of God, we want to be filled with his presence, we want to hunger and thirst for him in a way that changes our everyday lives. But how?

How do we find time and space for God in the midst of a world that fills our time, clutters our space, and offers so many substitutions for our hunger for God? How do we remember that God is offering satisfaction that lasts beyond the temporary filling we find in a trip to the mall, a bowl of ice cream, or an afternoon nap?

Life is full—often too full—and so many pressing, urgent things need to be done. Dinner must be cooked tonight, the kids have school projects due tomorrow, and—unless I want to go to work in my pajamas—the laundry has got to get done . . . now! We're ruled by time, and there never seems to be enough empty space on the calendar.

We want to make God the number one priority in life, but knowing God doesn't seem to have such an urgent deadline that we feel the need to meet it today or lose the opportunity. God is the same yesterday, today, and forever, and it stands to reason he'll be there next month or next year when life slows down.

I often find myself living in the future instead of in the present moment. I imagine that life will get easier next week, next month, or next year, and I'll find more time to do those things I dream of doing. I used to think, *I'll have more time for God when I quit my job and stay home*. But by the time that happened, Audrey hadn't yet learned to sleep all night, so I was always tired. Then I thought I'd have more time when Audrey started school, or when both of the girls were in school full time.

But we're one week into both of the girls going to school full time, and those empty days just waiting to be filled still aren't here. Sure, there are quiet moments throughout the day, but there's still laundry to be done, a house to be cleaned, a book to be written, and commitments almost every day of the week.

We long for a day when there aren't quite so many things on our to-do lists. Until then, it's so easy to put off God or even put off working out how to bring him into our moment-by-moment lives.

Yes, commitments end, appointments sometimes get cancelled, and time opens up for a moment. But it's quickly filled again with the next commitment, the next project, the next "next" thing. The truth is, there's really no such thing as empty space or time. Nature abhors a vacuum and so does the family calendar.

Still we have a nagging sense that if we could only figure out how to make God a priority, the rest of life would somehow improve. We'd find a hidden resource of patience and contentment and energy, as well as some certainty that what we're doing is really worthwhile. The problem is, figuring it out would take some time we just don't have.

I've often been left feeling discouraged, wishing for a different kind of life—the kind of life I imagine really godly women have somehow attained. A life filled with open space, where everything is just a little easier. A life where the only bumps in the road are small, where children are well mannered and do their homework when they're told. A life where marriage is always joyful and smooth. In other words, a life totally unlike the one I have.

Maybe it's just better to wait, I reasoned, *until I get it all together before inviting God into the messy details. Maybe I'm just not quite spiritual enough,* I thought as I'd try and fail to make him more central. *Maybe God doesn't really want to be part of my daily life,* I feared. *Maybe I'm just not good enough,* I concluded.

But Acts 17:26 says that God "determined the times set for them and the exact places where they should live." God chose the time and place for each one of us to live. And Psalm 139 tells us he knows each detail of our lives:

O LORD, you have searched me
  and you know me.
You know when I sit and when I rise;
  you perceive my thoughts from afar.
You discern my going out and my lying down;
  you are familiar with all my ways.
Before a word is on my tongue
  you know it completely, O LORD.

Psalm 139:1–4

If when and where we live, when we stand up and when we sit down, the words we think before we speak—if these aren't the stuff of daily life, I don't know what is. God knows *you* and God knows *me* and he wants to be in relationship with us in the midst of our *real* lives—not make-believe lives we dream of while in the midst of whichever chaos we happen to find ourselves. He wants to come into our lives and make a difference *now*; he's not waiting for us to get it all neat and clean before he'll come in.

Finding God in the Midst of Real Life

When we moved to California in 2003—away from family, friends, and everything familiar—my marriage fell apart. Toben told me he didn't love me, that he'd never really loved me. He disappeared for long stretches of time and was completely silent for days on end.

During the two years that followed, he was diagnosed as bipolar, suffering massive mood swings through various prescriptions as each medication was tried and failed. His alcoholism worsened, and there were days I doubted he'd come home.

Everything familiar was gone. Life changed from day to day. The only future plans I made were the "what if the worst comes to pass, and I find myself alone with two small children" kinds of plans. Would I stay in California? Would I move home to Colorado? Would I need to get a job? Would I want to get remarried someday?

In the midst of suffering, I found passion for God—a very real desperation for his presence in each and every moment. He was always there, of course, had always been there. But going through such a difficult time showed me the importance of giving him first place in my life, of making space for him to work. I learned that finding space for God was something I couldn't afford *not* to do. Spending time with him became the most important thing for my sanity, my soul, my survival. It might sound a little dramatic, a little overdone, but I learned the *only* way to make it through the day with any kind of success was with him.

It sounds backwards, but it's not through a life that's rosy and smooth that I understood God's desire to move in and take first place in my life. It was when my life was the messiest, most falling apart, most desperate. I simply could not wait until things got a little easier, a little neater to invite God into the everydayness of my life. Because, at that time, things just kept getting worse.

I figured that if God wanted to be part of my everyday, real life—if he could come in and make things new—then there was no time like the present. Instead of waiting for life to get better, maybe it was time to invite *God* to make it better.

God met me and ministered to me in a variety of ways during that time—through other people and their prayers and practical help, through a heightened awareness of his love and care for me, through his Word.

He met me and ministered to me *daily* during that time as I learned to set aside time for him and as I prayed to seek him first.

Things didn't improve right away—but slowly, day by day, life has returned to "normal." I praise God for the wisdom he gives doctors who create medicines that heal us. Toben is whole and healthy and full of hope.

God held us together, redeemed us from the pit. "He set [our] feet on a rock and gave [us] a firm place to stand" (Ps. 40:2).

I learned that giving God priority means that he is the one responsible for holding us together. My job is simply to hold on to him for dear life.

🏺   🏺   🏺

We *can* find God in the midst of our *real* lives—the lives we know we live but hope no one else sees clearly. We *can* walk through our days with him and make time with him a priority, and we can do it in the midst of a marriage crisis, babies who don't sleep through the night, doubts about our faith, and whatever else we're dealing with. God already knows the truth about our lives anyway, so it makes sense to approach a relationship with him from honesty.

In John 4, Jesus met a Samaritan woman at a well. Tired and thirsty, he stopped for a drink of water. She was there, and so he asked her for a drink. In the conversation that followed, this woman learned that it's no use pretending with a God who knows the truth of your life.

As they talked, the Samaritan woman tried to distract Jesus with arguments of when and where to worship God. Jesus responded by telling her that the place of worship isn't the point. What God wants is for us to "worship in spirit and in truth" (John 4:24). Pretending all's well may work—for a while anyway—with people, but not with God. As Beth Moore has said, we need to approach God from where we really are—from what we're really dealing with. If we're in the midst of crisis, we come from that. If we're in doubt, we come from that.[1]

Instead of pretending for now and waiting for life to be perfect later, be honest. "God, I don't have it all together and I'm tired of pretending I do. I want to make time with you a priority, but I don't have a clue where to begin or how to do it. I think you can improve my life, and I want to live each day in step with you. I've tried and I can't do it on my own. Help me!"

Where to Start

That's it. That's the start. When you invite God to help, he will. He's not pushy, not overbearing. He's going to wait until you ask before stepping in.

When we make spending time with him a priority each day, life does get better. That's the good news. Of course, your husband might not change, your problems won't automatically disappear, your children won't suddenly sleep all night long. But you will find a greater sense of purpose, resources beyond yourself, and a partner to walk with throughout the day. In other words, spending time with God will change *you*.

The bad news is—there's always bad news, isn't there?—it's going to involve making some changes, making some choices. And those choices may not be easy. Making God a priority and giving him space in our lives mean that other priorities may have to shift, and there might not be space for some other things. It may mean getting up earlier or staying up later, or giving up some time watching television on Monday nights. But we'll find that the fruit we gain from a deeper relationship with God far outweighs what we may give up.

Oh, and there's more good news—when we set out to find God, he is always waiting to be found.

As we get started, please keep in mind that the point of making space for God is not to check something off our spiritual to-do lists, to pat ourselves on the back and feel good about being "good" Christians. To paraphrase my friend and author Jan Johnson, the point is not great quiet times, but God-centered lives.[2]

Spending quiet time with God, then, is not an end in itself. Rather, it is a place to start. Our destination is to know God and learn more of him. The journey is in learning to carry that practice of fellowship and intimacy moment-by-moment into our living. Along the way, God can transform us into the likeness of his Son as we carry the light of the gospel into that part of the world in which we live.

Spending time with God each day can change your life. Not because of the behavior itself, but because the more time we spend with the Father, the more we take on his character as he teaches us and shapes us within the context of an intimate relationship.

Have you ever heard that couples who have been married for years and years start to resemble one another? Maybe not in looks so much (although I've seen some pictures that testify it can happen!), but in mannerisms, speech patterns, likes and dislikes.

That's how it is when we spend time with God. Day by day, little by little, his will becomes ours, his character our own. Our emotions will be moved by what moves his, we will become concerned by what concerns him, and we will become kinder, gentler, more patient.

In thinking about making a place for God, I came to realize something. Spending time with him is all about an invitation—his invitation to me, to you, to each one of his children.

This relationship, this time with him, isn't about obligation—something we do out of guilt or out of dread. When we start to see our time with God in light of invitation, the appearance of that time changes. As my friend Diana told me, "It has changed my perspective from viewing quiet time as an obligatory, guilt-ridden practice to an opportunity to be still and listen to his voice. Now my heart is full of adoration—I'm honored that he freely gives an invitation to me each day where we can share our hearts together."

This relationship together is *his* idea. He does the initiating, and he offers the invitation. And as with all invitations, we choose how to respond.

In the preface to one of the prayer books I use, the authors write this:

> We have given ourselves to the daily discipline and monthly retreats. Through it all we have discovered God to be an extravagant giver, a loving parent, whose every desire is to delight us and beckon us toward an ever closer walk with Christ.[3]

I love the words of Jesus in Matthew 11 as found in *The Message*:

> Are you tired? Worn out? Burned out on religion? Come to me. Get away with me and you'll recover your life. I'll show you how to take a real rest. Walk with me and work with me—watch how I do it. Learn the unforced rhythms of grace. I won't lay anything heavy or ill-fitting on you. Keep company with me and you'll learn to live freely and lightly. (vv. 28–30)

Did you get all that? It's one of those invitations I have to go back and read again and again in order to catch all that he's offering.

Am I tired? Worn out? What about you?

Am I burned out on religion? On the list of things to do, has religion become the instructions for how to do those things exactly right? Am I tired of checking off boxes and working at religion rather than developing relationship? Are you?

"Come to me," Jesus says. "Get away with me and you'll recover your life." I just love that. In my mind, I see him sitting beside the still waters of Psalm 23, patting the soft green grass next to him, beckoning me to stop running in circles and to flop down in the grass next to him.

It often feels, though, like we have to keep on running, keep on juggling, or life will come crashing down. Instead—somehow— Jesus says that the key to recovering life is to come to him. To learn from him "how to take a real rest." Really? It seems almost too good to be true. But then that's just how my Jesus is. Gentle. Kind. Tender.

He's not laying anything heavy or ill-fitting on me. He made me—he made you—and he knows what works best for us. "Walk with me," he says. "Work with me," he invites. He's right there to show us the next step to take, just how to live. He moves in those "unforced rhythms of grace" and slows down to show us how to move in the same rhythm.

And just when we get the rhythm down, he's not going to leave with a "You're on your own, kiddo." Nope. "Keep company with me," he invites. This is a journey, and he's with us every step of the way. And by keeping in step with him we "learn to live freely and lightly."

Oh how I want to live like that more and more! Don't you?

The choice between living a life that's forced and heavy or free and light is ours to make.

Making a place for God involves choice. If we want it badly enough, we'll make it. But as I said, making it may not be easy. Saying yes to God will mean saying no to something else.

It takes energy and determination to seek God first. It takes discipline and intention to turn to him first—to turn to him in the morning, in our responses, in our fear; for help, for wisdom, for advice, for answers; to share good news, when receiving bad news; for ideas and inspiration; for strength; in joy, in sorrow, in work, at play; in the quiet, in the chaos. To make God our "first" in everything—our preference, our favorite—means that we may have to change how we live, how we think, how we respond.

But with our eyes on the invitation—"Come to me"—with our focus on the goal—"Know me"—we can move forward one step at a time. We can make some hard choices here and there, knowing the joy that waits.

Learning to make hard choices is part of maturing, part of growing up in Christ. But at some level we know—our common sense tells us—those choices are necessary.

I love this quote (and I've used it often):

> Our lives can hold just so much. If they're filled with one thing, they can't be filled with another. We ought to do a lot of thinking about what we want to fill them with.[4]

If we're going to respond to God's invitation, we're going to have to decline some other invitations.

The good news is that God is a jealous god—he wants to be our number one priority. When we pursue him, he pursues us right back, increasing our hunger for him as we learn that we can be satisfied only in him.

When we are hungry for God, he promises to satisfy. "Open wide your mouth and I will fill it" (Ps. 81:10).

This fall, I was invited to talk to a group of women about God's invitation to meet with him. We talked about the invitation, about rest, about God's desire to meet with us. In closing, I asked each woman to close her eyes and listen to God's invitation to her. Each phrase, each word of this invitation is taken directly from Scripture. Listen to God's invitation to you:

My Child,
Come away with me by yourself
and get some rest.
Be still and know that I am God.
I will satisfy you with good things
and restore your strength.
I will waken you morning by morning

and I myself will teach you;
I will direct you in the way you should go.
My compassion never fails;
great is my faithfulness.
Wait for me.
Put your hope in me
and you will not be disappointed.
You are mine and I love you,
Your Abba

CHAPTER 1

Finding God

Grant that we may find You and be found by You.

I loved to hide when I was a little girl. My favorite places to hide were at the end of the piano tucked into a corner next to the wall, and under my bed. In both places, my mother (or my little sister) could come all the way into the room and never see me. I'd hold my breath and sit as still as possible, taking secret joy in knowing I was completely hidden and safe from discovery.

God does not hide from us, though, laughing when we can't find him. He wants to be found when we diligently seek him. I'm so thankful for that. Because that means finding God in the midst of my busy life isn't about searching under beds or in shadowy corners. If he hides at all, God hides in plain sight.

Scripture assures us that by his creation God has made himself known for all the world to see (see Rom. 1:20). The Bible also tells us that God is near to all who call on him (see Ps. 145:18). Sometimes seeing evidence of God involves simply looking up from ourselves and opening our eyes to what's right in front of our noses—the faces of loved ones, the flowers in the backyard, or the stars in the night sky.

That's where I see God in each day. I love God's Word for so many reasons—one of which is the pictures it paints of God's presence and the stamp of his personality on the world he's created. These pictures stick in my mind, so when I see something out in the world, it triggers thoughts of God.

I've scribbled notes and drawings throughout my Bible—
thoughts and ideas and prayer requests and underlining that
mean something special to me. In the book of Psalms especially,
I've drawn little smiley faces here and there—next to verses that
paint an especially vivid picture for me.

Here are some of my favorites:

> Sing to God, O kingdoms of the earth,
>   sing praise to the Lord,
> to him who rides the ancient skies above,
>   who thunders with a mighty voice.
>   Psalm 68:32–33

> Let heaven and earth praise him,
>   the seas and all that move in them.
>   Psalm 69:34

> He will be like rain falling on a mown field,
>   like showers watering the earth.
>   Psalm 72:6

> How glorious You are,
>   more splendid than the mountains.[1]
>   Psalm 76:4

> Mightier than the thunder of the great waters,
>   mightier than the breakers of the sea—
> the LORD on high is mighty.
>   Psalm 93:4

> Then all the trees of the forest will sing for joy;
>   they will sing before the LORD, for he comes.
>   Psalm 96:12–13

> Let the rivers clap their hands,
>   let the mountains sing together for joy.
>   Psalm 98:8

> He spreads the snow like wool
> and scatters the frost like ashes.
> He hurls down his hail like pebbles.
> Psalm 147:16–17

Can you see in these verses the pictures painted of God's presence?

Have you ever seen the clouds streak across the sky like God's chariot riding the wind?

Have you ever heard stones clatter in a river, sounding like applause for God?

Have you ever seen dolphins dance across the sea, smiling and filled with joy and praise for their Creator?

Have you ever stood in a forest as the wind comes up and seen the trees wave their arms to the sound of the wind's song?

Have you ever heard God's booming voice in the thunder— his declaration that he is the Almighty, the omnipotent God?

Learning to see God's hand in all things can take some practice. When I first began to wear contact lenses, I was excited to see clearly from dawn until dusk. But the doctor told me it would take some time for my eyes to adjust to my new lenses. He told me to wear them for an hour for the first day, two hours the next, slowly building up my ability to see in a new way.

For many of us, our desire is sincere to see God in each moment, be we forget it takes practice. We go through a day and then realize at bedtime that, after our quick morning prayer, we hadn't thought about God at all. *Oh no!* we think. *I've failed.* And when the same thing happens the next day, and the day after, with little or no improvement, we give up. *I'm not spiritual enough,* we reason. *This kind of thing is for people who are holier than me.*

Don't give up! God's Word, as well as history, tells of ordinary people—people like you and me—whom God used in extraordinary ways. Wives and mothers, widows and slaves, children and the elderly.

The story of Hagar in Genesis 16 fills me with hope. As Sarai's Egyptian servant, Hagar didn't merit much favor. Though she was pregnant with Abram's child, Abram told Sarai, "Your servant is in your hands. . . . Do with her whatever you think best." The verse goes on to say, "Then Sarai mistreated Hagar; so she fled from her" (v. 6).

Hagar was the mother of Abram's child, but her son would not be the promised heir. She was alone, pregnant, and afraid. No one cared for her—or so it seemed. Yet God called her by name, and she then called God by name, *El Roi*—"the God who sees me."

God found Hagar, and he finds you, too, that you may say with Hagar, "I have now seen the One who sees me."

What does it mean, though, to find God, to respond to his invitation to get away with him, to see his presence in our everyday lives? How do people in Scripture find God? What does God say about being found? How can we set realistic goals for finding God in the busyness of our lives?

Jeremiah 29:11 is a verse many of us have heard a lot. "'For I know the plans I have for you,' declares the LORD, 'plans to prosper you and not to harm you, plans to give you hope and a future.'" But the verses that follow have a lot more to say to us about finding God in the midst of our ordinary lives.

> "Then you will call upon me and come and pray to me, and I will listen to you. You will seek me and find me when you seek me with all your heart. I will be found by you," declares the LORD. (Jer. 29:12–14)

Do you want your future—starting tomorrow, starting now—to include a heightened awareness of God's presence in your life? Do you want to be filled with the hope of knowing he's right there with you? Call upon him—pray to him and ask him to fill you with an increased sense of his presence. Seek him with all your heart—give the pursuit of God your time, your energy, your best—and God himself declares that he will be found by you.

Where Is God?

So where is God? If we're going to find him, where do we start looking?

Theology tells us that God is omnipresent. The *Westminster Confession of Faith* explains it like this: "The whole or complete and infinite God is to be found everywhere at the same time."[2] In other words, God is everywhere all at once. Okay, that's helpful, but a little vague. In my search for God, I'd like more specific directions about where to begin.

As God's written Word to his people, the Bible is a good place to start. Simply opening the Word reveals the very nature and character of God as we read words that reflect his thoughts, his preferences, his standards. What, then, does God say in Scripture about where he can be found?

God Is Found in Praise

Psalm 22:3 says that God is "enthroned on the praises of Israel" (NLT). Don't you wonder what that looks like? And what it will be like to see that throne someday in heaven when we join with all the angels in singing, "Holy, holy, holy Lord, God of power and might, heaven and earth are full of your glory!"?

Music has power. Anyone who's had the Inspector Gadget theme stuck in her head—or the "I love you, you love me" song from *Barney*, or any other annoying tune for that matter—knows what I mean. When words are set to music, they stick in our minds, stay on our hearts, invade our thoughts at will.

What kind of music are you listening to? What's playing in your car? On your iPod? In the house? On the soundtrack that plays through your mind?

Don't get me wrong—I'm not suggesting that anything but Christian praise music is a sin. Not at all. But I am suggesting that what you listen to affects your thoughts, your attitudes, your emotions.

I can't tell you how much I have found this to be true for me. Listening to great praise music that stirs me to worship God and praise his name makes a huge difference in my day. Cleaning house can be a time of grumbling about the kids who left toothpaste in the sink, the husband who didn't rinse out the tub, and the cat who tracked litter through the bathroom—or it can be a time to praise God and find his presence in the midst of my everyday chores. Finding him there means something as mundane as housecleaning becomes an act of joyful service for my family.

Running errands can be a time of hurry and worry, racing from one thing to the next, complaining about the slow driver ahead of me. Or it can be a time to praise God and find his presence in the midst of daily errands. With my mind focused on who God is and the greatness of his power, I look up to see the mountains near my home and recall Psalm 121:1–2, which reminds me to "lift up my eyes to the hills" and that "my help comes from the LORD, the Maker of heaven and earth."

Please don't think I'm some kind of superwoman, cleaning house each day with a song in my heart like some kind of modern-day Snow White. Like you, I have days filled with complaints, days when I'm irritated and short-tempered. Days when God seems distant and hard to find.

But choosing to praise him in the midst of the humdrum and ordinary tasks of my day makes a difference. *Choice*. That's the key. Some days more than others it's easier to choose to praise. But that's where the rubber hits the road—for those days when it's hard to choose what's best are when I need to chose what's best the most.

In a Bible study I recently went through, Beth Moore talked about God and his plans for us. He doesn't want to change just your life, she said. He can change your day! And not only that, she went on to say, God can even change your mood.[3] Now that's good news!

What are you doing today? How might praising God in the midst of it change your attitude and transform the mundane into time spent with the Creator?

A way this plays out in my life is in my morning walks. Walking the dog each day (well, almost each day!) is pretty mundane and ordinary. But since Toben bought an iPod for me, my walks have changed completely. I put on some great praise music (Kirk Franklin, anyone?) and sing my heart out. I'm sure it looks a little nuts to the neighbors, and I try to tone it down when I see someone coming. I do sometimes have an awkward moment when I turn a corner and come face to face with someone while I'm belting out a hymn. I smile and say good morning, and hurry on my way!

The forty-five minutes Daisy and I spend walking the trails in the neighborhood have become more than just exercise and fresh air. Instead, that time becomes worship, energizing my soul and fixing my focus on God for the day. A walk with Daisy becomes more—it becomes a walk with the Creator through his creation.

God Is Found Where His People Gather

In Matthew 18:20, Jesus told his disciples, "For where two or three come together in my name, there am I with them." What an incredible statement! It's one of those things I know to be true, but at the same time can't quite wrap my mind around. How incredible that Jesus would be present with us when we gather in his name.

The "two or three" makes me stop and think. I know that God has promised to never leave me or forsake me (see Heb. 13:5), but this statement from Jesus makes me realize how much I need other people. I'm not an island; I can't go it alone. When I feel like God is distant, when I'm having trouble practicing his presence, I need the help of others.

And that's why believing friends are so precious. Having a friend to whom you can turn in all honesty and beg for help in making God seem more real is an incredible gift. Have you ever felt low and all alone, only to find that the company of Christian friends lifts you up, refocuses your attention? How wonderful it is to meet with a friend and invite Jesus to meet with you. To talk about all he's done and is doing in your life, to be encouraged and to encourage one another.

That's likely one of the reasons the writer of Hebrews admonishes us not to give up the habit of meeting together (see 10:24–25). He knew that when we meet together in the name of Jesus, God comes near.

For the past year, I've been meeting with a group of women to pray. We get together on Thursday mornings in a small conference room down the hall from the teachers' lounge at school. We sit around the table and invite God to come and meet with us as we talk about the school, our children, and share prayer requests. The little room has become holy ground—and our small group has become tightly knit as we've found comfort in God's presence and in one another.

Where else, though, do God's people gather? In addition to small groups of friends who gather in God's name, church is an obvious place to find a gathering of God's people.

Throughout Scripture we see a time and a place set aside for God's people to meet in his name. From the book of Exodus, where the people met in the tabernacle, through the kingdom of Israel and Solomon's temple, and to the book of Acts when believers met in homes—"church" is a place to find God.

My friend Sarah had this to say about attending church:

> I've attended church off and on. I went back to church a number of times because I felt that God's people are called to gather, and I wanted to be in a place where I would be challenged and able to grow.
>
> My pastor talks a lot about Jesus coming to change hearts—that there will be real world change when hearts change. It has made me look at all the ways that Jesus asked us to change our hearts, and consider how my heart needs to change. So you could say my relationship with God has changed, that I have accepted that God put us here to learn things, and I am paying more attention to what those things might be.

I can identify with Sarah. I find that attending church, spending time with other believers, helps me to pay more attention to what God is teaching me.

With whom are you meeting? With whom do you spend your time? I'm not advocating leaving unbelieving friends out in the cold—by no means! But when I'm struggling to find God in the midst of my daily life, meeting with other believers brings him near. I can complain to a friend, or gather in Jesus' name. Once again, the choice is up to me. And the choice is up to you.

Choice is a funny thing. I like having choices, but often what I should choose and even want to choose, I have a hard time choosing. I feel like Paul, who wrote in the book of Romans:

> I do not understand what I do. For what I want to do
> I do not do, but what I hate I do. And if I do what I do

not want to do, I agree that the law is good. As it is, it is no longer I myself who do it, but it is sin living in me. I know that nothing good lives in me, that is, in my sinful nature. For I have the desire to do what is good, but I cannot carry it out. For what I do is not the good I want to do; no, the evil I do not want to do— this I keep on doing. Now if I do what I do not want to do, it is no longer I who do it, but it is sin living in me that does it.

So I find this law at work: When I want to do good, evil is right there with me. For in my inner being I delight in God's law; but I see another law at work in the members of my body, waging war against the law of my mind and making me a prisoner of the law of sin at work within my members. What a wretched man I am! Who will rescue me from this body of death? Thanks be to God—through Jesus Christ our Lord! (7:15–25)

Can you relate?

I'm with Paul—thanks be to God. I can call to him for help, and he comes to my rescue, enabling me through the Spirit to make good choices.

God Is Found on His Throne in Heaven

> The LORD is in his holy temple;
> the LORD is on his heavenly throne.
> Psalm 11:4

"Our Father in heaven," begins the Lord's Prayer. God is every-where—all at once, all the time. And one of those places is heaven.

To realize this, I often have to look up. Beyond myself, beyond my circumstances. No matter what's going on around me or in me, God is above it all. He knows it, he's sovereign, he's in control.

Look up. God spoke these words to me the other day. Not in a loud voice that others could hear. It wasn't really a voice at all, I suppose. But that morning as I walked through the neighborhood, out of nowhere the words were so clearly imprinted on my heart.

Look up, God said. Not at my feet, at the boring and dull gray road. Look up—to the trees, to the blue sky, to the world around me.

How often do we keep our eyes cast down, mired in the circumstances of our day, feeling hopeless and lost and defeated? Too often, likely. In Psalm 3:3, David called God the "lifter of my head" (AMP). Why does God lift our heads? One reason is so that we can look up and see him!

Look up! For that is where God can be found. On his throne, in control, and sovereign in all the details of life that press us down. Look up, and see things from God's eternal, perfect perspective.

David writes again in Psalm 123:

> I lift up my eyes to you,
>> to you whose throne is in heaven.
> As the eyes of slaves look to the hand of their master,
>> as the eyes of a maid look to the hand of her mistress,
> so our eyes look to the Lord our God,
>> till he shows us his mercy.
>
> vv. 1–2

Look up to see what God is bidding you to do in whatever situation you find yourself. Look up to see God, whose throne is in heaven. Recognize that God is your master, and we cannot follow closely until we look up to see what he is doing, where he is leading.

As I thought about this idea of looking up, I was surprised at how often it shows up in Scripture. God told Abraham to "look up at the heavens and count the stars" (Gen. 15:5) to show Abraham the scope of God's promise. Later, Abraham looked up to see the ram caught in the bushes, God's provision for a sacrifice in place of Isaac (Gen. 22:13). When Isaac was grown, Rebekah looked up to see him, and they fell in love and were married.

Joshua looked up before the battle of Jericho and saw the commander of the army of the Lord (Josh. 5:13). The people of Beth Shemesh looked up to see the ark of God being returned from capture by the Philistines (1 Sam. 6:13). King David looked up to see the angel of the Lord with a sword stretched toward Jerusalem (1 Chron. 21:16). Through Isaiah, God urges us to lift our eyes and look up to the heavens, to consider the God who created the stars (Isa. 40:26).

Jesus, too, looked up toward heaven as he broke bread and fish to feed the multitudes (Matt. 14:19). He looked up again when he prayed to raise Lazarus from the dead (John 11:41). Mary Magdalene and Mary the mother of James looked up to see the stone rolled away from the tomb on Easter morning (Mark 16:4). Stephen looked up to heaven and saw the glory of God as he was stoned to death (Acts 7:55). And at the end of time, we shall look up to the heavens: "Look, he is coming with the clouds, and every eye will see him, even those who pierced him; and all the peoples of the earth will mourn because of him. So shall it be! Amen" (Rev. 1:7).

But the picture that stands out most to me is from Ezekiel. I smiled and even laughed out loud when I read this passage:

> In the sixth year, in the sixth month on the fifth day, while I was sitting in my house and the elders of Judah were sitting before me, the hand of the Sovereign LORD came upon me there. I looked, and I saw a figure like that of a man. From what appeared to be his waist down he was like fire, and from there up his appearance was as bright as glowing metal. He stretched out what looked like a hand and took me by the hair of my head. The Spirit lifted me up between earth and heaven and in visions of God he took me to Jerusalem. . . . And there before me was the glory of the God of Israel. (8:1–4)

Can't you just see it? There's Ezekiel, sitting in his house surrounded by the elders of Judah. I imagine it was hot, a little stuffy, and voices were droning on and on. His head is nodding as he stifles a yawn, then God shows up and grabs him by the hair. "Ezekiel! Look up here!" The pull on his hair forces him to look up beyond his surroundings. And there he sees "the glory of the God of Israel."

Sometimes I need God to grab me by the hair and to lift my head, to help me look beyond my circumstances, beyond the ordinary to see him and his glory. He seems to say, "Joanne! Look up! Look at me!"

Yes, Lord, help me look up—even if you have to wreck my hairdo to do it.

God Finds Me

I was raised in the Presbyterian church. Calvinistic theology with its ideas of predestination and the chosen elect are part of my background. I learned the acronym TULIP to remember the five points of Calvinism—total depravity, unconditional election, limited atonement, irresistible grace, and perseverance of the saints. I could recite them offhand. A mouthful of theology for sure.

But what you believe about the doctrines of free will, the elect, or predestination, isn't the issue when it comes to finding God. When we look to the pages of Scripture and read stories of how people came to know God, we see that God always sets out to find us first.

It was God who appeared to Abram and called him out of Ur to the Promised Land. It was God who called out to Moses from the burning bush and revealed his plan to free his children from slavery in Egypt. It was God who called out to the persecutor Saul on the Damascus road and changed him into the apostle Paul.

God always finds us first.

Psalm 139 is a psalm that I recite for my children. It's comforting for them to know that God never sleeps, that he watches over them, that no matter where they go—to a friend's house, a new classroom at school, a move to a new town—he knows right where they are. He never looks around frantically, wondering where they are. He knows. They are never lost.

That psalm comforts me, too. While at times I may look around, feeling like God has suddenly disappeared and that I'm all alone, it's just not true.

The words of David attest to the truth that God is there—and knows me through and through.

> O Lord, you have searched me
> and you know me.

You know when I sit and when I rise;
 you perceive my thoughts from afar.
You discern my going out and my lying down;
 you are familiar with all my ways.

Psalm 139:1–3

When we are saved and are found in God (Phil. 3:9), he is with us even "to the very end of the age" (Matt. 28:20)—whether or not we feel like that's true. And that's the crux of finding God for us, to move beyond our ever-changing feelings to the truth of Scripture. Immanuel has come—God is with us. With me and with you.

My prayer for myself and for you is that finding God will be not so much about *feeling* in tune with him in our day-to-day lives. Rather, finding God is about training ourselves to look to the truth of his presence, to embrace practices that open our eyes to that truth, rather than doubting his truth because it doesn't feel like he's here today.

My feelings are fickle. They just are. I can swing from one extreme emotion to the other—and feel everything in between—in almost no time. It's exhausting, isn't it?

The prophet Jeremiah had it right: "The heart is deceitful above all things and beyond cure. Who can understand it?" (17:9). Who indeed? So often I don't even understand my own emotions, my own feelings, my own heart.

There is, though, an answer to Jeremiah's question. *God* understands my heart. He knows me, loves me, and understands me.

Yes, I want to love God and to experience an emotional relationship with him in my heart and soul. But the relationship must also involve my mind. Paul writes in Romans 12:2 that we are to be "transformed by the renewing of [our] mind[s]." We cannot rely solely upon our feelings when it comes to our relationship with God.

R.S.V.P.

Something that helps me respond to God's invitation is recognizing things that get in the way of my response. Those things that distract me and steal my focus away from God.

Here are a few of my distracters:

- Worry. When I'm "worried and upset about many things" like Martha in Luke 10:41, I have a hard time sitting still with God.
- Self-absorption. Being focused on myself and my wants and my needs makes it hard for me to listen to God.
- Busyness. When I fill my days to overflowing, I'm tired, grumpy, and feel like "I just don't have time" to sit down with God.
- Careless intake. When I fill my mind with "worthless things" there's little room left in me for God and his Word.
- My own stubborn refusal to pay attention. Ouch! Sometimes I'm just bound and determined to ignore God's invitation. I'd rather flit about than sit still and listen to what he has to teach me.

What about you? What are some things that get in the way of your saying "yes" to God's invitation? Knowing the things that get in the way helps us recognize them when they appear—and helps us take steps to get back on track sooner rather than later.

Take a few minutes and identify what distracts you from God. Make a list, if you're like me and love lists. Then stick it in your Bible, on the bathroom mirror, on the fridge—someplace where you'll see it throughout your day. Those things *will* pop up to distract you from responding to God. Being aware of them and on the lookout will help you recognize and deal with them.

On the flip side, I sat down and thought about those things that bring my focus back to him, that help me respond to God's invitation.

Here's a few things that put my eyes squarely upon God:

- Seeing every task as a task done for God. Colossians 3:23 says, "Whatever you do, work at it with all your heart, as working for the Lord, not for men." As I go through my day, seeing my tasks as being done for him sets my mind on him so I'm ready and more willing to meet with him each morning.
- Having a reminder to refocus. For example, every time I walk by the place where I meet with God, I'm reminded of what I studied that morning.

- Listening to music is huge for me. I mentioned this before, but having a background of praise gives me a hunger to go and meet with God.

Your turn again. What might help you refocus throughout your day? Are there one or two things that you could use as reminders to get your focus back on God? Make another list (or add to the previous one), and put it someplace where you'll be sure to see it.

We find God in many places—in praise, in the company of other believers. But one other place where we find God is in quiet time spent alone with him. As in any relationship, it takes time together to develop intimacy, to get to know one another. It's great to spend time with him among other people—but there's something special about time alone.

I love spending time with Toben in the midst of family and friends, but I also need time alone with him—just the two of us. A different dynamic works when we're alone; conversations happen that don't happen when other people are around. Intimacy needs some time that's exclusive.

In the same way, we find intimacy with God when we respond to his invitation to come away with him alone.

Like any good host, God has a plan in mind when he invites us to meet with him. What's on the agenda? What plans does he have for us?

The rest of this book takes a look at what it means to meet with God alone and in quiet. What it is, why and how we do it, how God uses it to change us into the image of his Son.

CHAPTER 2

Finding a Purpose

*You satisfy us with good things,
and our strength is renewed.*

Quiet time is a phrase most of us have probably heard again and again. Yet, though I've been a Christian for most of my life, it's only been in the past few years that the practice of setting aside time for God has stuck.

I went through phases of having a quiet time—it was something my youth pastor talked about a lot and something I felt I *should* do. But it was hard to find the time in high school when school started just after 7 AM, and harder to stay awake at night after I got home from my job, finished my homework, and talked on the phone with my best friend. In college, too, the practice stuck for a while—but never for very long. Then came marriage, and starting a career, and then starting a family. Here and there I'd find time to read and pray, but it never lasted for more than a month or two.

But in the past few years, setting aside time for God has become a habit, and I can't go for more than a few days without it. Spending time with God has become a necessity for me. And after years of meeting with him almost every day, I can't imagine *not* finding time to spend alone with him.

A daily appointment with God has become part of my morning routine—as automatic and natural as pouring that first cup of coffee or brushing my teeth. I know what a day without that appointment looks like—and it's not pretty. It's far worse than caffeine withdrawal!

What has made the difference?

Simply put, my purpose has changed. Time with God is no longer something I do out of obligation or guilt or any of those other reasons we're often given for spending time with God. Instead, I spend time with God in order to know more of him, this God who went to such extraordinary lengths to make himself known to me.

Other benefits come, of course, as a result of spending time with God. Peace and joy and love and the other fruit of the Spirit are sown, watered, and grown during that time with God. Spending time with God helps me order my days, evaluate my priorities, and approach tasks with a new perspective.

But let's start with the basics. What is a "quiet time" and why have one?

What Is Quiet Time Anyway?

Quiet time is one of those phrases used a lot in Christian circles. But what is it exactly and what does it really look like? Those are good questions—especially when time is something we never seem to have enough of. And quiet? What's that?

I said it at the beginning—having a great quiet time each day is not an end in itself, our spiritual practice that's a sign we have arrived. Instead, it's where we get in step for the journey of walking in fellowship with God in each and every moment.

I'm sometimes tempted to think, *I can do that without having quiet time.* I'm especially tempted to do without it when it's dark and cold and it seems like the alarm goes off way too early. Maybe so. But if I'm going on a journey with someone, and if we're to travel together, we've got to meet somewhere and begin together. We must agree on a place and a time. Together we look at the map, together we determine how we'll get to our destination, together we go.

Quiet time is that time and place. Spending time in the Word is the map. Listening and learning and putting into practice what he's taught me is the journey.

Quiet time, devotions, Bible time—whatever you want to call it—it's time spent alone with God. And here's the incredible thing—God wants to spend time with you! He's the one who invited us into relationship with him, and he's the one calling us away to be with him.

Could You Use Some Rest?

One reason he wants to be alone with you is to give you rest. Could you use some of that today? I sure could—in fact, I could use some of that each and every day!

We find such an invitation in the words of Jesus, found in Mark 6:31: "Come with me by yourselves to a quiet place and get some rest." What an invitation! The disciples had just come back from being sent out by Jesus. They'd traveled from place to place—they'd "preached that people should repent. They drove out many demons and anointed many sick people with oil and healed them" (vv. 12–13). Then look at what happened:

> The apostles gathered around Jesus and reported to him all they had done and taught. Then, because so many people were coming and going that they did not even have a chance to eat, he said to them, "Come with me by yourselves to a quiet place and get some rest." (vv. 30–31)

Have you ever felt the way the disciples must have felt? As women, I think we get the picture! Maybe a paraphrase for women would go something like this:

> The women gathered around Jesus and reported to him all they had done—caring for husbands, teaching their children, going to work, volunteering at school, preparing meals for a neighbor, helping at church, caring for elderly parents, helping with homework, driving kids to dance and soccer and piano, doing some laundry, cooking dinner, settling arguments between kids, and cleaning house. Then, because the whole family was coming and going so much that

these women didn't even have a chance to eat, Jesus said to them, "Come with me by yourself to a quiet place and get some rest."

Jesus said essentially the same thing in the well-known words of Matthew 11:28–29: "Come to me, all you who are weary and burdened, and I will give you rest. Take my yoke upon you and learn from me, for I am gentle and humble in heart, and you will find rest for your souls."

And here's something really cool I just learned. The Greek word for rest in this verse is *anapauo* (pronounced an-ap-OW-o). It's a compound word, made from *ana* and *pauo. Pauo* means to cease, to give rest. Pretty straightforward. But here's the part that jumped off the page at me—*ana* means again.

The kind of rest Jesus is offering to us is rest that we need again and again. It's not a Band-Aid kind of rest, a one-time-for-all-time kind of rest. He wants us to come back to him again. Whenever we find ourselves weary and burdened, we come again to him for rest.

Oh, he knows us so well, doesn't he?

All too often, we treat rest as just that—a once-in-a-while kind of thing for when life gets *really* out of control. So we go to bed early one night, instead of setting a realistic bedtime every night for ourselves and for our children. Or we spend time with a friend once in a while, instead of making time for friends a regular practice. We plan a two-week vacation (and promptly get sick when we slow down!) in hopes that it will sustain us for the other fifty weeks of the year, instead of making time to rest each week, each day.

"Come to me, all you who are weary and burdened, and I will give you rest," Jesus invites.

What's your answer to such an invitation?

My answer? Yes, please!

Instead of just one more thing on the to-do list, spending some quiet time alone with God gives us rest. It's an opportunity in the midst of each hectic day just to be still and know that he is God (see Ps. 46:10).

"Learn from me," Jesus said. What do we learn from his life

here on earth? He, too, needed time alone with the Father, away from the hustle and bustle of his busy ministry. Again and again, the Gospels show Jesus slipping off for some quiet time with the Father.

Luke, a physician by trade who knew the body and its functions, notes this: "At daybreak Jesus went out to a solitary place" (Luke 4:42). Jesus was tired. The day before he had taught in the synagogue, then gone to the home of Simon and healed his mother-in-law. Then as the sun set, "The people brought to Jesus all who had various kinds of sickness, and laying his hands on each one, he healed them" (Luke 4:40). Sounds exhausting.

And the next morning at daybreak, Jesus went out to a solitary place. Mark 1:35 tells it this way: "Very early in the morning, while it was still dark, Jesus got up, left the house and went off to a solitary place, where he prayed." Jesus prayed and met with the Father. He needed rest that sleep alone could not provide.

Satisfaction, Anyone?

Rest isn't the only benefit of spending some quiet time alone with God.

Have you ever had one of those days when you feel just a little off? Dissatisfied, but not sure what you need to give you satisfaction? I have. I wander through my day, trying a little of this, a little of that, but nothing quite does the trick. I feel vaguely uneasy, out of tune with the world, and on edge with everything and everyone I meet.

I've found that having a daily appointment with God—quiet time first thing in the morning—gives me satisfaction. It meets my needs before the day begins and frees me to then meet the needs of others.

In Psalm 90:14, Moses, "the man of God" as he's identified, prayed this prayer: "Satisfy us in the morning with your unfailing love, that we may sing for joy and be glad all our days."

I love this verse.

In God we can find satisfaction. We don't need to experiment with different things in different amounts to find what we need. All kinds of analogies point to this kind of experimenting. We're hungry but not sure what we're hungry for, so we eat little bits of this and that without getting exactly what we want. We leave the pantry full but unsatisfied. Or, we try to fill that God-shaped void with shopping and relationships and whatever else we can think of—and nothing fits quite right.

What do you do to find satisfaction? As women, we often look to busyness to fill the void. The more we have on our plate, the more satisfaction we think we'll find. We say yes to this and yes to that, and fill our days and lives and closets and cars to over-flowing—and then wonder why we still feel empty when we stop and sit still for a moment.

And so we keep going and keep doing, and avoid quiet and solitude for fear we'll find ourselves face to face with dissatisfaction. It becomes a never-ending cycle—being too busy to stop, too busy to make time for God, too busy to notice what's missing.

I recently came across this quote again from Brennan Manning's book, *Abba's Child*:

> Our controlled frenzy creates the illusion of a well-ordered existence. We move from crisis to crisis, re-sponding to the urgent and neglecting the essential.[1]

When I read that quote for the first time years ago, I under-lined it and wrote in the margin, "My whole life!" That described exactly how I felt. But as I read the quote today, it's no longer the case. As I've journeyed toward simplicity, toward making room for the essential, the frenzy has gone. With time set aside for God, pursuing an intimate relationship with him my primary goal, sat-isfaction has become the norm rather than the exception.

Sure, there are still crazy days. I live in the real world, have real kids, a real husband, real concerns. But the satisfaction I've found in God has proved trustworthy in the face of whatever life brings my way.[2]

The truth is that nothing—no thing—material can fill our im-material souls. Only God can give us satisfaction.[3] Our satisfaction is *always* met in God. He is what we're longing for, and he's ready to meet our needs. "Open wide your mouth and I will fill it" (Ps. 81:10).

God satisfies us right away when we ask. Remember Psalm 90:14: "Satisfy us *in the morning* with your unfailing love, that we may sing for joy and be glad all our days" (emphasis added).

There's no need to wait for satisfaction until later on in the day when things have started to unravel. God is ready and willing to give us satisfaction first thing. Before we run around looking for substitutes that don't work, we can find the kind of satisfaction that will make us glad for the rest of the day.

God's love is unfailing. He always shows up when we come to meet with him. We're never left waiting around, looking at the clock and wondering if we've been stood up. He has promised to be found when we seek him with all our hearts. And God always keeps his promises—hallelujah!

And once we're satisfied, we can "sing for joy and be glad all our days." Because our deepest needs have been met in God, we're free from looking to our husbands, our children, our friends to give us satisfaction that can only be found in God. We can approach others in freedom and without unrealistic and unvoiced expectations. And because we've found satisfaction in God, we can let that flow out of us into the lives of others.

Finding Intimacy

As in any relationship, we need one-on-one time in our relationship with God so that intimacy can grow and develop. It's great to worship God in the fellowship of a church setting, it's wonderful to study the Bible with a group of women. But God loves *you*—and wants to spend time alone with *you*.

Have you ever been jealous for time alone with your husband, your best friend, or your child? You've spent time together in larger groups with lots of people around and lots of activity happening. But you're longing for some time just to sit face to face and really connect. God is jealous for that kind of time alone with you. He is El Kanna—Jealous God—and sometimes he wants you all to himself.

God's jealousy is not the petty jealousy of humankind—the kind that makes us discontent with our lot because we want what someone else has. His jealousy pursues us as objects of his desire—he wants us to be wholly his. "He is a Lover who will not be satisfied until we return his love with equal passion," writes Ann Spangler as she defines this name of God.[4]

As I studied this name of God several years ago, I became more aware of God's pursuit of me—and thankful for his jealousy for me. His jealousy doesn't stifle, doesn't trap. Instead, his jealousy is what causes him to pursue the lost.

The picture of Jesus as the good shepherd comes to mind. It is his jealousy for his own that makes him leave the fold and pursue the lost sheep—the one alone and afraid. I don't know about you, but from time to time my attention gets distracted from God, and I get lost in a maze of busyness and crisis. I need God to come and bring me home again.

I found this prayer in my journal from that study: "El Kanna, my Jealous God, Thank you for being jealous on my behalf, for pursuing me . . . I confess my wandering, my distraction. Please pull me back and pursue me when I start to stray . . . You are my God—be my focus, my passion, and my goal."

In her book, Spangler pointed out how English poet Joseph Addison described jealousy: "Jealousy is that pain which a man feels from the apprehension that he is not equally beloved by the person whom he entirely loves."[5]

I don't think God is up in heaven biting his nails over whether we'll love him. He doesn't force our love. He has gifted us with choice. And he woos and waits for us to choose him.

We can't learn to love him as he loves us if we don't spend time getting to know him in an intimate way.

I looked up *intimacy* in the dictionary. Here's what stood out for me. Intimacy involves a loving, personal relationship. Intimacy has an element of privacy about it. Intimacy includes feelings of belonging, of closeness, of friendship.

Belonging, closeness, friendship—all of these require us to be real, to be authentic. As we talked about in the last chapter, there can be no pretending with God if we want intimacy in our relationship with him. So we come to him—alone and in private—honest about who we are and who he is. And intimacy begins to grow.

I love what my friend Susan wrote a couple of months ago on her blog:

> I had so gotten away from Him. There was no intimacy. Little contact. An occasional wave as I ran by on my way to "My Busy Life."
>
> We all know that when this happens, He brings our busy life to a screeching halt. Praise Him, He did that with me . . .
>
> Bring it to Him every morning. And I don't mean just in the flowery, little devotions either. They are all good. I do them. I love them. But I'm talking
>
> Bring.
>
> It.
>
> The joy, the sadness, the worry. The anxiety, the praise, the worship.
>
> Bring it . . .
>
> I have got to bring it to Him every morning. Or I'm lost.[6]

Her brave honesty reminds me that this is what God wants from me. To be free to be real. To be who I really am. And to be loved in response.

Seems a little unreal, doesn't it? A little too good to be true? That we could be who we really are—at the core, deep down on the inside—that we can open up that place that nobody else sees, and that God won't turn away, but instead will come and embrace us. The possibility of it leaves me breathless. The truth of it moves me to tears. That he loves me like this makes me come undone. Do you know that he loves you like this? How I pray you do.

Each and every time we come to him alone and in private, in authenticity and transparency, this is his response. Love like no other.

Isn't this the heart of the gospel?

An Open Invitation

Are we commanded to spend time alone with God? Is there a verse that says, "Thou shalt have thy quiet time"? Sometimes it seems like there must be. But what does the Bible actually say?

I looked and looked for a command to have a quiet time in my Bible, and it's just not there. What we do see is the *principle* of time set apart to meet with God acted out again and again in the pages of Scripture.

In 2 Timothy 3:16–17 we read, "All Scripture is God-breathed and is useful for teaching, rebuking, correcting and training in righteousness, so that the man of God may be thoroughly equipped for every good work."

Everything we need to know to live life well is found in Scripture—either spelled out exactly or demonstrated in principle. So while no specific chapter and verse commands spending time with God, the principle is demonstrated.

We see Adam and Eve in the garden with a regular time to meet God. Genesis 3:8 says that they "heard the sound of the LORD God as he was walking in the garden in the cool of the day." They had a practice of meeting together, and God kept that appointment and expected Adam and Eve to do the same. "Where are you?" he called when Adam and Eve hid.

God waits to meet with us and seeks our company. And that makes a huge difference in how we approach our time with him. Here's what a dear friend of mine had to say about her knowing that God wants to meet with her:

> In the last year, I've learned—through Bible study, prayer, and through others—that God is all about re-lationship. A relationship with *me*! Imperfect, sinful, selfish, angry me. To know that, to remember that every day, compels me to respond to His seeking.
>
> I have never been a morning person. I'm techni-cally still not (in my mind, anyway), but I know that if I do not crawl out of my warm, snug, and cozy bed before the darlings get up, I will not meet Him in the sanctuary (physical as well as spiritual). I may come to Him grumbly and sleepy and nursing my second

cup of coffee, but He always meets me there! Never grumbly, never tired. Always patient and loving.

Knowing that He is waiting for me to get up to pray, to listen, to study, to seek him, to have a relationship with him is such an incredible comfort to me.[7]

Knowing this—that God wants to meet with us—changes our response. Take a look at what another friend had to say, "It has changed from an obligatory guilt-ridden feeling to a heart full of adoration and sheer honor that he freely gives an invitation to me each day where we can share our hearts. It's become a time that I don't want to miss!"

God wants to meet with you, too.

Moses climbed the mountain to meet with God. And other times he entered the tabernacle where "the LORD would speak to Moses face to face, as a man speaks with his friend" (Exod. 33:11). I want to meet with God face to face, as with a friend. I long for heaven and the opportunity to do just that.

The closest I can come now is to use my imagination each morning when I meet with God. I sit on the couch and pray aloud, as if God were sitting in the chair opposite me.

I love the story that Brennan Manning tells about an old man dying of cancer. He set up an empty chair in his hospital room for Jesus, and prayed by talking to that empty chair each day. When he died, his daughter reported "something strange, beyond strange, kind of weird."

She said, "Apparently just before Daddy died, he leaned over and rested his head on a chair beside his bed."[8]

I want to "see" God as clearly!

The psalms are full of David's reflections on meeting with God as well as his encouragement for others to do the same. "Be still before the LORD and wait patiently for him," he wrote in Psalm 37:7. God has promised to come; we can wait in expectation.

As we saw earlier, Jesus himself set aside time to spend with the Father. And he invited others to do the same—to get away with the Father and find the rest they need.

Why did all these people spend time alone with God? Because he invited them to spend such time with him. God doesn't force us to sit down and be still with him. Instead he extends to us an invitation.

The parable comes to mind about the man who sent out invitations for a banquet. The parable begins,

> A certain man was preparing a great banquet and invited many guests. At the time of the banquet, he sent his servant to tell those who had been invited, "Come, for everything is now ready."
>
> But they all alike began to make excuses. The first said, "I have just bought a field, and I must go and see it. Please excuse me."
>
> Another said, "I have just bought five yoke of oxen, and I'm on my way to try them out. Please excuse me."
>
> Still another said, "I just got married, so I can't come." (Luke 14:16–20)

When I was a child in Sunday school I remember singing a song about this story. "I've married a wife, I've bought me a cow."[9] These words sound silly, but we adults come up with similar excuses not to accept God's invitation to go and meet with him.

God is inviting you and me to spend some time alone with him. Isn't that incredible? The God of the whole universe is inviting me to sit down alone with him! He's inviting you as well—offering you his undivided attention, his time, his presence. It's almost too incredible to believe.

What's my excuse not to meet with God?

Am I trapped in the cycle of the urgent, rushing from one thing to the next without pausing for rest? Am I overcommitted and too busy? Do I need to stop and think about what's really important to me, to decide what's most valuable and then structure my time and priorities around those things?

There are plenty of excuses—reasons that responding to God's invitation gets pushed lower on the list. But we all find time to do the things that are important—sleep, read to our kids, get the grocery shopping done. Maybe we need to slow down and recognize the magnitude of his invitation.

What's your excuse not to meet with him?
"Come away with me," he whispers.
What will your answer be?

Quiet Time Is Good for Us

The ultimate reason God invites us to spend quiet time with him is because he knows it's good for us. As my heavenly Father, God knows I need quiet in my day. He knows me well, and knows that my tendency is to overdo, to overcommit, to run myself ragged. He knows I need time alone with him to rest, to learn, to be still, to be loved.

When my children were small, quiet time was part of our day. From one until three o'clock each afternoon we turned off the television, took the phone off the hook, and were quiet. By taking that time in our day, we had the energy we needed to have fun together for the rest of the day. Without quiet time, life got grumpy and nobody had any fun.

Some days they willingly took a quiet time without arguing. They knew they were tired and needed rest for whatever came later. Other days, they felt fine and didn't want to stop what they were doing. "Do we have to?" they'd whine.

They ultimately learned to trust that I knew best and had their best interest in mind. They accepted that I knew more about what they needed than they did.

I'm amazed at how often I see myself in my children! Do I trust that God knows best, that he knows me better than I know myself? Do I believe that he knows more than I do about what I need? Will I go to quiet time willingly or whining?

A Healthy Start

Having quiet time with God in the morning permeates the whole day. Just like eating a healthy breakfast is essential for our bodies, spending quiet time with God in the morning is essential for our spirits. It's easy, though, to cross it off our lists and move on without a second thought. So, in your time together with God, ask him to remind you during the day of the time you spent together.

During the day, when feelings of unrest or dissatisfaction arise, we can remember that God met those needs already. I've said it before—feelings aren't always reliable. When I'm feeling dissatisfied, I have to renew my mind by remembering that God is my satisfaction, that he has already met my ultimate need for the day. As I meditate on that truth, then my feelings begin to fall into line.

Having a quiet time gives us a chance to practice throughout the day what we learned. I need him, though, to take those lessons learned in quiet and help me put them into practice in the course of my day. I want what he teaches me to be put to the test, to be proved real and useful and reliable.

The other morning the gospel reading in my prayer book included the parable of the persistent widow.

> Let those who would seek continue seeking until they find.
>
> This is the way of the kingdom—
>
> There was a woman who, no matter what anyone else said of her, continually confronted a judge for vindication in her case. Time and time again, she knocked at his door and pleaded for justice. The judge cared neither for justice nor for the woman, but finally he gave in. Because even though what was right or wrong did not bother him, she did.
>
> Ask and you will receive, I tell you; seek and you will find; knock and the door will open wide before you. The door will always be open to one who knocks.[10]

I scribbled in the margin: "O God, help me to persevere, I pray. So often, I confess I give up when answers don't come right away. Remind me, please, keep things in my mind so I keep seeking, keep asking, keep knocking."

I thought a lot about how easily I sometimes take *no* for an answer. I realized that if I'm not persistent in prayer for some things, maybe it's not something I really want. Or maybe it's just laziness. What are some things I'd prayed about in the past and given up on? Salvation for friends and unbelieving spouses, healing for the sick, encouragement for the discouraged. I was ashamed to see how quickly I'd given up. How would perseverance in prayer have made a difference? I thought about that question throughout the entire day, and it has affected my prayers since.

R.S.V.P.

Quiet time is a loaded phrase. It means different things to different people. How would you define "quiet time"?

Take some time to think about it. What are the images, ideas, or feelings that come to mind when you think about quiet time?

Is quiet time something you do or have done in the past? What has worked for you? What hasn't worked? What have been your challenges when it comes to spending time alone with God?

One of the reasons quiet time is important is because God wants to give you rest. Stop and think about that. What is making you weary these days? Are you treating rest as a once-in-a-while kind of thing, using random moments of rest as a bandage on a larger problem? In addition to finding rest in God, are there other changes you need to make in order to be rested? Are you going to bed too late and getting up too early? Do you have open time on your calendar, or are your days packed to overflowing?

What about satisfaction? Where are you looking for satisfaction—in God, in others, in family? What have you done to fill the void? Is it working? How might finding satisfaction in God free you in your relationships with others?

And, finally, what about intimacy? Is your relationship with the Father close and intimate—or do you spend time with him only in crowds? How does it make you feel to know that God is jealous to spend time alone with you?

Are you authentic with God? Do you pretend that things are fine when they're not? How could you approach God in honesty?

At times I've felt awkward when telling God that I'd rather stay in bed, that I'm feeling grumpy, that my heart's just not in what I'm reading or praying. But the more I think about being authentic, about nurturing intimacy in our relationship, the more I realize that since he knows the truth, I might as well acknowledge it. Once it's out in the open, once I stop pretending about whatever *it* is—we can deal with it together.

What does it mean to you that God waits to meet with you and seeks your company? Does knowing he's *inviting* rather than commanding change your view of time spent alone with him?

Put yourself in the parable of the banquet. God has issued an invitation to you. What are the things that get in the way of saying *yes?* Are you so caught up in the urgent that the important is getting neglected?

As Susan said earlier in the chapter—bring it. Take your frustration, your busyness, all those things that get in the way of your time together—and lay it at the feet of the Father. Tell him about it and ask him for wisdom. Work on it together.

You may like the sound of what you've been reading so far, but you may be thinking, *I can see that quiet time is good for me and something that can make a difference in my day. But* how *do I do it?*

That's a good question. The chapters that follow talk about the practical, nitty-gritty details of how to accept God's invitation for quiet time with him. Where does a quiet time happen? What do we do during a quiet time? What part does prayer play in a quiet time? What if we get bored or it becomes a dull routine? And how does the practice of quiet time then permeate our day and our lives?

More good questions. Let start looking for some answers.

Finding a Place

In the morning when I rise, give me Jesus.

Where are you going to meet with God each day? *When* are you going to meet with him? Those are two important questions to answer if quiet time with God is going to happen.

The first question is probably easier to answer. Where are you most comfortable? Where can you be alone, in quiet, without having to worry about being disturbed?

The kitchen counter, the couch, in bed. The kitchen table, the back porch, the living room. A porch swing, on a run, in a big comfy chair by the fireplace. The answers are as different as one person is from another.

Where I spend time with God changes from time to time. It depends on the season, the home I live in, the weather outside. For a while, I sat at the dining room table, looking out into the backyard as the light dawned and the birds began to sing. For a time, I sat in the kitchen, tucked into a corner and wrapped in a blanket.

In the cold of winter I like to sit in front of the fireplace. In the time leading up to Christmas, I sit in the living room as the tree lights twinkle. During the summer, I love the cool mornings on the back deck.

The couch, my favorite chair, in bed if my husband is away, even walking the dog through the neighborhood—all of these places have been space for God and me to meet. All are ordinary places, but made sacred because of God's presence and the time we share there.

Some things never change—no matter the location (except for the walk—it's hard to read and walk at the same time!). Coffee is a must—milk added until it's just the perfect creamy color. My Bible and a pen. If I'm inside, the dog is almost always snoring at my feet and the cat purring on my lap. I usually have an assortment of books piled on the table or floor around me—from my Bible study homework to a prayer book to whatever else I happen to be reading at the time.

It sounds ideal—and it is. But it's taken me awhile to get here. I've had plenty of mornings—and still do—when the cat chases the dog, knocking over the *hot* coffee onto my lap and Bible. Or mornings when I've overslept and my quiet time doesn't happen at all. Mornings sometimes get interrupted by sick children, vacation schedules, and whatever else gets in the way. But after years of meeting God each day, my routine *usually* works pretty well.

Where Shall We Meet with God?

Where do we see people in the pages of Scripture meeting with God? Do these places share anything in common? Can they guide us in our own choice of where to meet with the Creator?

As seen in the last chapter, Adam and Eve met with God in the garden of Eden, and they walked together in and among the trees. Nature was their setting for meeting with God. For them, activity and conversation went hand in hand.

Moses set aside a specific place. The purpose of the Tent of Meeting was a place to go and meet with God. And while we only read of Moses and Joshua entering the tent, it was available to anyone who wanted to inquire of the Lord.

> Now Moses used to take a tent and pitch it outside the camp some distance away, calling it the "tent of meeting." Anyone inquiring of the LORD would go to the tent of meeting outside the camp. And whenever Moses went out to the tent, all the people rose and stood at the entrances to their tents, watching Moses

until he entered the tent. As Moses went into the tent, the pillar of cloud would come down and stay at the entrance, while the LORD spoke with Moses. Whenever the people saw the pillar of cloud standing at the entrance to the tent, they all stood and worshiped, each at the entrance to his tent. The LORD would speak to Moses face to face, as a man speaks with his friend. Then Moses would return to the camp. (Exod. 33:7–11)

As Moses entered the designated place of worship, God came to meet with him in a cloudy pillar. Did you notice *how* they met? "Face to face, as a man speaks with his friend." Now that's the kind of quiet time I want to have!

Daniel, too, had a specific place to pray:

Now when Daniel learned that the decree had been published, he went home to his upstairs room where the windows opened toward Jerusalem. Three times a day he got down on his knees and prayed, giving thanks to his God, just as he had done before. (Dan. 6:10)

Daniel's response to God's invitation was a given. He didn't wonder each day if he would meet with God or where he would meet with God. The question for Daniel was never *if* he would meet with God. "Just as he had done before." Daniel's practice had been repeated until it was part of his habit—a given in his day. It was something you could, in fact, almost set your clock by—the officials of the day knew exactly when and where to find Daniel.

In Jesus' ministry of traveling and proclaiming the good news of the coming kingdom, he didn't have one place to go and meet with his Father. But the places he went were all isolated and set apart. Luke 5:16 says, "But Jesus often withdrew to lonely places and prayed." And at the very beginning of the gospel of Mark, we read this:

Very early in the morning, while it was still dark, Jesus got up, left the house and went off to a solitary place, where he prayed. Simon and his companions went to look for him, and when they found him, they exclaimed: "Everyone is looking for you!" (Mark 1:35–37)

Jesus and the Father are one—yet they still set aside time to meet together.

I think it's worth noting that Jesus took such time alone even when "everyone" was looking for him. Sound familiar? We as women, wives, and mothers often feel like "everyone" is looking for us, wanting something from us. Even when everyone has needs to be met, though, we need time away, time alone with God to give us direction and energy for when everyone finds us.

And in reality, there should be a little time every day when there aren't needs to be met—early in the morning, after everyone goes to sleep at night, when the kids are at school or taking a nap. Again, it's the excuses, the endless reasons that keep us from acknowledging that we *can* take time away with God.

When the girls were tiny, I often used nap time as time for myself—to read a book, to watch a movie, to catch up with friends. I had the time to meet with God but chose not to. I wonder what "could have been" if I'd made meeting with God a priority. Would I have been a better mother? What would God have taught me in that time and space?

In *Prince Caspian*, Aslan constantly reminded the children no one ever gets to know what would have been:

> "Please, Aslan! Am I not to know?"
> "To know what *would* have happened, child?" said Aslan. "No. Nobody is ever told that."
> "Oh dear," said Lucy.
> "But anyone can find out what *will* happen," said Aslan. "If you go back to the others now, and wake them up; and tell them you have seen me again; and that you must all get up at once and follow me—what will happen? There is only one way of finding out."[1]

We don't get to know what would have happened. But how

wonderful that we can find out what *will* happen—if we get up and follow him where he leads.

The story continues as Aslan asks Lucy to do just what he has said—to get the others and follow him. To urge them to follow—even though they might not believe her, might not see Aslan. In fact, when Lucy asks if the others will see him, Aslan replies, "Certainly not at first. Later on, it depends."[2]

How true this is as we follow God, as we encourage others to follow him, too. They may not see him at first, they may not believe us at all. But the only way for them to find out what will happen is to take him up on the offer and follow.

And it's true for beginning quiet time too. Others can tell us the benefits, show us the path, testify to the results. But we won't really know for ourselves unless we try it.

Creating Sacred Space

Sacred space is not a new idea. It's a space made special by the presence of God. Like the conference room where I meet other mothers to pray, it's space that may appear ordinary but has been made holy.

Toben has visited a camp outside of Kansas City where dozens of sacred spaces have been created on their large property.[3] Some are as simple as a bench in a clearing, while others are more ornate. One of the favorite spots at camp is an old, abandoned cellar on the edge of the property. Half a dozen steps transport you down into a small, stone-walled room with sawdust on the floor and a cross on the wall. Benches are scattered here and there for people to sit and pray and be silent with God.

Many religions have a concept of sacred space—whether a formal church or an obscure marker in the countryside. Judaism and Christianity are no different.

Moses' Tent of Meeting, the tabernacle, and the temple were sacred spaces for the Israelites living before Jesus. Under the new covenant in Jesus, *we* are the temple. Paul writes of this in 1 Corinthians 6:19 when he says, "Do you not know that your body is a temple of the Holy Spirit, who is in you, whom you have received from God?"

And in John 14:23, Jesus told his listeners, which includes us today, "If anyone loves me, he will obey my teaching. My Father will love him, and we will come to him and make our home with him."

Incredible, isn't it? That God would make his home with us—frail, sinful, fallen people who have become the redeemed. While I know it's true that the Spirit dwells in me, having a physical place to meet with God is important to me. It helps me become focused in my quiet time.

I love this idea of creating sacred space in order to meet with God. It's not so much about adding on a room or redecorating. Any place can be sacred space if that is where we seek God. Sacred space is simply a place dedicated or devoted to the sacred. It's set apart for a specific purpose, set apart as special.

This prayer of Brother Lawrence is a good one for women:

> The time of business does not with me differ from the time of prayer; and in the noise and clatter of my kitchen, while several persons are at the same time calling for different things, I possess God in as great tranquility as if I were upon my knees at the blessed sacrament.[4]

A noisy kitchen, full of people all talking at once? Sounds like a seventeenth-century monk might have something to say to a twenty-first century woman! Who knew?

My husband and I were talking about sacred space the other morning as we walked through our neighborhood. "It's like Carmel," he said. "It's a place that's more than just a place to us. It has special meaning for us—a place that recalls our relationship, romance, and memory."

It's true. Carmel for us is more than a place on the map. It's where we spent our honeymoon, and where we celebrated our anniversary for many years after. It's a place filled with story, with memory, with purpose.

And a couple of years ago, it became a place for our family, too. Toben decided it was time to include the girls in this sacred space, and surprised us with a trip to Carmel for Thanksgiving. He told us what to pack and how long we'd be gone, checked us into our flight online, and kept us away from the gate until the last minute, when we learned where we were going.

He's pretty incredible!

It was so fun to introduce Audrey and Emma to some of our favorite places—a leisurely drive along the Seventeen Mile Drive through Pebble Beach; the beach at Asilomar, where you can always find starfish; afternoon tea at the Cypress Inn; the Christmas decorations along Main Street.

And we added new places as well—Carmel Valley Ranch, where we ate Thanksgiving dinner and watched wild turkeys run all over the hillside; the Rodgrigue Studio, which is home of Blue Dog, a favorite children's book character, and where Emma learned not to touch paintings in a gallery.

Do you have places like that in your life?

The place you choose to meet with God can become such a place. Set apart, consecrated, devoted to intimacy with your Father and Savior.

I love what one woman told me:

> Until recently I hadn't applied a specific time or place [for my quiet time]. I rearranged my furniture in my living room and soon discovered that a rocking chair had become my designated place. This chair was given to me by my mom, and it has been in our family since I was small. . . . Sometimes I sit in this chair other times of the day, and when my two children see me there they comment on how Mommy is having time with God.[5]

It's not that we determine that a specific location has suddenly become sacred. Rather, it becomes so over time. The practice of meeting God there adds something to it—until even others recognize its importance.

The kitchen table, a special chair, the front porch swing, the bath tub, in bed, on a walk or run, in the car on your morning commute—all of these places where women meet with God can become sacred, set apart. Nothing fancy, nothing too special at first look—but made holy by God's presence.

When Shall We Meet with God?

When are you going to meet with God?

Like any relationship, if you don't make specific plans, it's hard to make the relationship a priority, to make time together happen. "Let's get together for lunch," a friend says in passing. "Soon," you respond. But if you don't make plans, weeks go by and then months until you run into one another again. "We really should get together," you say. "Yes, let's do it soon," she responds. And so it goes.

Chances are, if you don't pick a *specific* time to meet with God it's not going to happen. You want to meet with him, you want to make it a priority. But if you don't set a specific time to do it, other things will crowd in, and you'll fall into bed night after night, thinking, *I really meant to meet with God today. Tomorrow will be different.*

I think that sometimes we use God's omnipresence—his being everywhere all the time—as an excuse not to get specific when it comes to meeting together. But, once again, our relationship with God is just that—a relationship. And for us to meet, we need to be deliberate.

Here's a simple truth it took me way too long to learn: If you don't set the alarm, you won't get up early. Sounds pretty basic, huh? Here's some of the other basic stuff that has helped me so much: Decide *where* you'll meet with God. Set out your Bible and whatever else you may need the night before. Fill the coffee maker so all you have to do is push a button. Do yourself a favor and make it as easy as possible for yourself!

Wait a minute, you're thinking. *You're talking about early morning again.*

Yep.

There's a good reason, I promise. Keep reading.

Seek *First* the Kingdom

The psalms are full of references to meeting with God in the morning. Take a look at just a few:

In the morning, You hear our voice;
    early we begin our watch for You.
             —from Psalm 5

We will sing of Your strength
    and celebrate Your love each morning.
             —from Psalm 59

It is good to give thanks to You,
    to sing praises to Your Name.
It is good to tell of Your love in the morning,
    and Your faithfulness at the close of the day.
You have made us glad;
    we shout for joy at the work of Your hands.
             —from Psalm 92

Let us hear of Your love in the morning,
    for we trust in You.
Show us the road that we must walk,
    for we lift our souls to You.
Teach us to do what pleases You,
    let Your good Spirit guide us.
             —from Psalm 143[6]

Like David, I'm convinced that there's no better time to start the day with God than at the start of the day. Giving God first place means meeting with him *first*—before the rest of the day gets going. Even Jesus got up early—while it was still dark, even—to go and meet with God. It's not easy, but as I often tell my kids, lots of things worth doing are hard at first—math, writing in cursive, playing the piano.

Before you start thinking that you hate mornings, let me encourage you. *Early* means different things to different people. By early, I mean *first* thing. I'm not saying you need to set your alarm for 5 AM and creep downstairs in the dark, yawning and tripping over the cat.

Our lives are all different. Some of us are married, some are not. Some of us have children, some do not. Some of our children are older, some don't yet sleep through the night (how well I re-member that!). Some of us need to be at work by eight, some of us don't get up until eight.

My friend Angie is a total night owl. We've joked that we live our lives on completely opposite schedules. But here's what she had to tell me: "On the very *rare* occasions I have gotten up early and started the day with the Lord . . .what a difference! I have more patience with my family, a lighter heart, greater focus, a sense of purpose." And so she's taking what she calls "baby steps" toward the goal of mornings with God.

This practice of quiet time with God isn't about comparing ourselves with others. We're not doing this to impress others, to set the bar and make sure others measure up.

Quiet time is about meeting with God. You and God, spending time alone together. It's not about me, your friend, your neighbor down the street, or your pastor's wife.

Jesus said, "Seek *first* his kingdom and his righteousness" (Matt. 6:33 emphasis added). In terms of my day, *first* means before my day gets going with its tasks, worries, and plans. I don't know when your day begins, and it doesn't really matter. What matters is that it begins (whatever the clock says the time is) with seeking God first.

During the school year, that's early in the morning for me. My girls need to get up and out the door for school each day. And how our morning goes affects their day at school. (I learned that one the hard way!)

For me to help them set a good tone for the day ahead, I need to have my focus set, my priorities in place, my satisfaction met *before* they get up. When I've spent time with the Father, reading and praying and committing my day and my children to the Lord, I can approach them with patience and help them turn their focus to God as well.

At this stage in our lives, in this season of back to school, I need to get up early. It's not always easy—especially as the weather gets colder, the mornings get darker, and I'm warm under the covers. But I've learned that not getting up and seeking God is far worse than my bare feet hitting the cold floor—grumpy mornings and grumpy girls (mom included) are the result.

Summertime, though, is a whole different story. I still get up before everyone else—but only because they stay up later in the summer and sleep much later on summer days. Even at that, the girls often come padding down the stairs before my time with God is finished. But without a morning deadline of walking out the door at a certain time, I can be more flexible.

Even if it's just a few minutes, set aside time to commit your day to him; that's seeking him first. Your schedule may be different from mine or your best friend's. In fact, I have a friend who spends a few minutes with God first thing, and comes back for more time later in the day when she's fully awake and her schedule is more open.

What season of life are you living now? Is it summertime, filled with lazy mornings in your pjs before heading off to the pool, or do you need to get everyone up, dressed, fed, and out the door on time? Do you have others living in your house—people whose schedules affect your own—or do you have space and time to yourself?

I say it again: your quiet time is yours. It doesn't have to be at the same time as someone else's.

I had lunch with a friend yesterday. We sat on her deck in the autumn sunshine and talked about the necessity of quiet time with the Lord. "Are you still getting up early?" she asked me. I told her about back to school, about the new routine we're still adjusting to after the open flexibility of summer. And I asked her about her schedule.

It's completely different from mine. Janna's daughter is not quite two years old and can't get dressed alone or find her own breakfast. My friend is pregnant, and her growing body requires an increased amount of sleep. On most days, Janna is just getting up as my kids and I are heading out the door.

Does it matter that I'm up hours before she is? Not at all. The thing that matters is that when her day begins, it begins with God.

Teaching by Example

Does quiet time have to happen before anyone else is up? Not necessarily. My friend Marla admits, "My ideal 'quiet' time is when none of my kids are awake. But they're always up before I'm completely done." As a result, she says, "There are a lot of interruptions for diaper changing, breakfast-making." That's just how life goes sometimes.

I can relate. There are times when I get up later than usual and hurry through my time with God, all the while listening for the sound of little feet upstairs. But I'm learning—slowly—to relax and to realize that having my kids come downstairs before I'm finished isn't a bad thing. In fact, it can be a *good* thing.

Children learn by example. And seeing me in the Word each morning, head bowed in prayer, is good for them to see. Just last week, my youngest daughter Emma came tip-toeing downstairs. "Mama?" she whispered. I looked up. "Can I pray too?"

She climbed up onto my lap and followed my finger across the page of my prayer book. I read the words out loud, pausing for her to read the "sight" words she's learned so far.

Most all of us hope that our children will learn to make time with God a priority. The primary way they do so is by watching us do it.

I love hearing from mothers of young children who don't wait for the "perfect time" to spend with God. Quiet can be all too fleeting in a home with young children. Instead, they gather their babies in their arms while they pray, or scatter toys at their feet for their little ones to play with. They remember the words of Jesus and are not shy about "letting the little ones come unto him" as part of their time with God.

Why Seek Him *First*?

God knows what's best for us—and if he says to seek his kingdom *first* there must be a good reason. While I know and believe this, I still find myself asking why. So why seek him first with quiet time each day?

Decide Who Will Be the Boss

For one, I think seeking God first establishes who's boss. Joshua told the people of Israel, "Choose for yourselves this day whom you will serve" (Josh. 24:15). While Joshua may have been talking about a once and for all choice as the Israelites faced life in the Promised Land, I hear in his words a challenge to the choice I must make each and every day.

Whom will I serve *this* day? The choice is there each and every morning. And it's mine to make. Will I serve myself—my own selfish interests, my own desire to do only what I want to do? Or will I serve God? Will I seek his will and direction for this day? Will I be open to go where he leads, even if it's not what I was expecting?

As the girls and I drove to school the other morning, we prayed as we usually do—for the teachers, the students. We thanked him for the beautiful day, the mountains to the west. When it was Emma's turn, there was silence. "I don't really have anything to say today," she said. "You said it all already."

I explained, "Well, if nothing else, you could tell God that you will let him be the boss today." She could tell him that she wanted to follow him, to obey him, to serve him as she went about her day in first grade. "Deciding now—on the way to school—that God is boss," I told her, "means that when you're tempted to disobey or do something wrong, you can remember that you already made your choice to obey."

Establishing who's boss is one reason to seek God first. Along with that, seeking God first begins the day on the right track. It's much easier to have a clear picture of where you're going, getting on the right path as the day begins, than to change course halfway through the day.

Get Your Needs Met

We've already talked about the idea that having quiet time with God brings us satisfaction. Seeking God first—being satisfied first thing in the day—frees us up in our relationships with others right from the start. Our needs have been met—before we come into contact with anyone else—so we're ready to serve without needing others to somehow fill us up. Take a look at Psalm 62:5–8:

> Find rest, O my soul, in God alone;
>   my hope comes from him.
> He alone is my rock and my salvation;
>   he is my fortress, I will not be shaken. . . .

Trust in him at all times, O people;
pour out your hearts to him,
for God is our refuge.

When I look to other people or the circumstances of my day to find rest, hope, or salvation, I'm guaranteed to be disappointed. My husband can't fill those kinds of needs, neither can my family or my friends.

God alone is the one who can "meet all [my] needs according to his glorious riches in Christ Jesus" (Phil. 4:19). Did you catch that? He can meet *all* my needs. *All* your needs. No matter what they are.

And there's more. I love the part of the verse that says to "pour out your hearts to him" (Ps. 62:8). He's the ultimate listening ear and shoulder to cry on. How might the shape of your days change if you poured out your heart to God first thing? What if you got everything off your chest *before* you're tempted to dump on the people around you, bringing them down and perhaps saying something you'd later regret?

Try it. Just take everything on your heart and pour it out to the Father. Lay it all down at his feet, take refuge in him, and then start your day. I bet those around you notice a difference.

Number Your Days

Back to the prayer of Moses found in Psalm 90. Before Moses asked God to "satisfy us in the morning with your unfailing love" (v. 14), he asked God for something else.

"Teach us to number our days aright," he prayed in verse 12, "that we may gain a heart of wisdom." I tend to be a literal girl. And so when I saw that the Hebrew word for number means "to count, reckon, assign, appoint," I realized that Moses is asking God for help with his calendar, his to-do list, his appointments for the day.

I have a calendar, a to-do list (well, several actually), appointments for today. Do you?

Part of walking with God is walking with him throughout our days. And not just days like Sundays when we're occupied with church. But *every* day. Days filled with laundry and errands and meeting friends for coffee. With work and playing with our kids and cooking dinner.

So quiet time first thing is an opportunity to plan your day with God's help. What needs to be done today? Who might you need to call with a quick word of encouragement? What's most important on your list?

Ask God to teach you as you number each day, and you'll be surprised at how he responds. Often he puts someone on my heart, and so I pray or send a card, only to discover that God somehow used that to make a difference in that person's day. Or I'll call just to say hello and find there's a need to be met.

One woman told me that planning her day with God makes a huge difference: "Without that early morning time, I feel like I'm just in reaction mode all day long," she said. "When my days start with him, my days feel more proactive, and I feel on top of things."

As believers, we have the awesome privilege to be God's hands and feet as he works through us in the lives of others. Numbering our days with him makes us available and on the lookout for such work as we pray with Isaiah, "Here am I. Send me!" (6:8).

Enjoy the Silence

I don't know about you, but I crave stillness, quiet, and calm— something that can be hard to find in the midst of children, music, vacuum cleaners, televisions, phones, friends, and family. All good things but they do make noise. Sometimes I just need everything to stop and be quiet.

Can you relate? Do you go through the day hoping for a moment to sit still, to be quiet? Do you ever fall into bed at night and realize it's the first quiet you've had all day? *Starting* the day with God means you get some peace and quiet each and every day.

"Giving God what I have left at the end of the day is such a sad amount to give to such a great God," my friend Wendy wrote to me awhile ago. She ended the message with this: "I am going upstairs and setting the alarm! I'll keep you posted."

A week or so later I received another message from Wendy. Here's what she said: "I have had the most amazing week of waking up early to pray. God has met me in so many amazing ways, including the fact that my kids have started getting up an hour later than they did just a week ago!"

I'm not promising that he'll do the same with your kids. But God wants to meet with you, and he's going to help you do it!

Sounds pretty good, huh?

One reason I love my quiet time so much is that whatever the day brings, I've had some time to sit still and be quiet. It charges my batteries, fills my reserves, and gives me energy to get going with my day without worrying whether there will be some time for *me*.

"I started getting up ninety minutes before my family a few months ago," one woman told me. "I absolutely love that time. The house is so dark and quiet."

Let's face it. We all need some downtime in our busy days. When I don't get it first thing, I get more and more tense, more and more on edge as the day goes on. I find myself resenting my children when I sit down for a minute and they interrupt, or getting frustrated when the phone rings.

I don't want to live my days tense, resentful, and frustrated. Having time with the Father first means I'm free to meet the needs of my family and simply be grateful if there are a few minutes of quiet later on.

Quiet Time *Every* Day?

When I consider the benefits of quiet time, I realize that I want it each and every day. And let's be honest—it's something I *need* each and every day.

In the Old Testament, the people of Israel offered sacrifices each day—morning and evening—at the Tent of Meeting, their sacred space. While we don't offer these kinds of sacrifices today, take a look at what it involved and how God responded:

> This is what you are to offer on the altar regularly each day: two lambs a year old. Offer one in the morning and the other at twilight. With the first lamb offer a tenth of an ephah of fine flour mixed with a quarter of a hin of oil from pressed olives, and a quarter of a hin of wine as a drink offering. Sacrifice the other lamb

at twilight with the same grain offering and its drink offering as in the morning—a pleasing aroma, an offering made to the LORD by fire.

For the generations to come this burnt offering is to be made regularly at the entrance to the Tent of Meeting before the LORD. There I will meet you and speak to you; there also I will meet with the Israelites, and the place will be consecrated by my glory.

So I will consecrate the Tent of Meeting and the altar and will consecrate Aaron and his sons to serve me as priests. Then I will dwell among the Israelites and be their God. They will know that I am the LORD their God, who brought them out of Egypt so that I might dwell among them. I am the LORD their God. (Exod. 29:38–46)

Their offering was a regular practice, a daily occurrence. And in their practice we see that it was pleasing to God. In this time of sacrifice he met with them, spoke to them, and consecrated the place with his glory. He promised to dwell with them, be their God. "They will know that I am the LORD their God," he said.

How does this apply to us today?

Romans 12:1–2 says this about the sacrifice we offer as believers in Jesus Christ:

Therefore, I urge you, brothers, in view of God's mercy, to offer your bodies as living sacrifices, holy and pleasing to God—this is your spiritual act of worship. Do not conform any longer to the pattern of this world, but be transformed by the renewing of your mind. Then you will be able to test and approve what God's will is—his good, pleasing and perfect will.

We offer our whole selves to God in worship. Each and every day. Jesus taught us to pray for our *daily* bread in the Lord's Prayer. And from Scripture we know that "man does not live on bread alone but on every word that comes from the mouth of the LORD" (Deut. 8:3).

I want the word that God has for me today. Do you?

I can tell a difference when I miss my quiet time. I've discovered that three days without the bread of God's Word is about my limit. After that, I find myself starving for God. Days one and two I feel vaguely off, but by day three I'm grumpy, unsettled, and not very nice to be around!

It took me awhile to link the cause and effect together, but I've tested it and it's true. I need what God has to offer in our time together. He knows me, knows what I need, and knows I can't live very well without it.

I'm not the only one who has made this discovery. Many women have found it to be true. They need their time with the Father. "My life is totally different," said Susan, "when I'm actively committed to my daily quiet time. Period." Betsy said, "I can always see a difference in my thoughts and actions when I'm consistent with my quiet time." "If I don't have my quiet time," said Sara, "I feel out of touch with the Lord and my family."

Not only that, it can make a difference for the rest of the family, too.

"Mornings that I've taken time to put God first, setting the tone for our home," said Janna, "my daughter wakes up content, happy, and ready to meet the day. Days I miss it, she seems to be whiney and demanding right off the bat. Some of this is probably in my attitude, but I *know* there is more to it than that—because I can see the difference as soon as I walk into her room!"

I love what Amanda Jones wrote on her blog about the *daily* practice of quiet time: "Hard times come and go, hormones rise and fall. But when the foundation of daily surrender and the filling of the Spirit are there, getting through the day is a lot easier and more enjoyable. Now can I get an Amen?"[7] (Can you tell she's Beth Moore's daughter?)

Amen, indeed!

R.S.V.P.

Time for the nitty-gritty details. If you're a planner like I am and love to make lists, this is what you've been waiting for. If not . . . well, you're probably thinking, *Here she goes again!* But this is where the rubber meets the road.

Make a list—on paper, in your head—but spend some time thinking about these things. You have to *choose* to meet with God and take some steps toward making that choice a reality.

- What does it mean to seek God *first*? What things tend to come first in your day? How would seeking him first change your routines?
- Is there time in your morning routine to meet with God?
- Do you need to get up earlier (or go to bed earlier!) in order to make some time to seek God first?
- Where will you meet with God? Is there a place where you feel most relaxed and comfortable? (I know some women can do this in bed—but I'm *too* relaxed and comfortable there!) How can this spot become sacred space for you?
- Do you need coffee, tea, something to eat in order to function properly and concentrate?
- What can you do the night before to make the morning easier? I need to prepare the coffee, make sure the family room is picked up, and clean up the kitchen. Facing a sink full of dirty dishes first thing is too overwhelming for me, and I just can't concentrate!
- Are there particular areas you need to determine ahead of time, areas where you will obey God? I have some challenging people in my life—chances are you do too. When those people cross my path and I'm faced with the temptation to act selfishly or unkindly, I need to have determined ahead of time that I'm going to follow God in that difficult situation.
- As part of meeting with God, ask him to help you number your days. Go through your calendar, your to-do list with the Father. Ask him to show you the path you should take in your day, to make you aware of how to serve him as you journey from morning until night.

Just do it! Pick a place, pick a time, and go for it. But don't just take my word for it. Listen to what one woman, Meredith, told me: "I wish I had started having quiet time earlier in my life. I would encourage everyone to start doing this on a *daily* basis. The results far exceeded my expectations."

I agree with her wholeheartedly. What I've gained from daily quiet time—rest, intimacy, soul satisfaction—far outweighs anything I've given up in exchange.

Deciding what things you'll need for your quiet time and what you'll do in your quiet time is next.

CHAPTER 4

Finding
a Practice

It is true that unless we have some method,
we shall assuredly lose the very best results.

The place where I meet with God changes from time to time. So does what I do in my quiet time. It can take some time to find the right practice—and once found, it can still change and develop into something different depending upon the season and the amount of time set aside to meet with God.

I've tried all kinds of things in my quiet times. Five minutes of prayer, reading the Psalms or the book of Proverbs in a month, working my way through the Gospels, reading a devotional, writing in a journal, simply being quiet. Different things have fit best at different times in my life.

Part of the reason it has changed is because the amount of time I spend each morning has changed. At times it has been a few minutes before jumping into the shower, at other times ten minutes of quiet before everyone else gets out of bed, or half an hour of silence, or a day or two on retreat.

What are you going to do in your quiet time? Read, write, sing, pray. Be still. Listen. What's most appealing to you at this point in your life?

If you're just beginning, pick something small and simple. I sometimes have the tendency to go a little overboard when I start a new project, setting myself up for possible failure. (Thus the king-sized quilt that's been *almost* done for the past seven years. I do plan to get it done this winter—really.) If you decide to spend an hour reading Leviticus every morning at 4:30, you may burn out and quit.

Do you love poetry? Start by reading a psalm every day. Are stories more to your liking? Try a gospel, or maybe an Old Testament book like Esther. Love music? Listen to a hymn or praise song and sing it out to God. Do you like to write? Grab a journal and write a prayer to God each day.

My friend Holly keeps a prayer journal in which she records prayer requests and their answers. She has a separate page for different members of her family, for friends, and Christian leaders for whom she prays. "I got a new one this year," she told me, "because the old one was so used it tore in two!"

Other women have told me that they journal so they can go back and see God's faithfulness—especially on days when they're feeling stuck or blue. One woman said, "It reminds me of where I've been and where God has taken me."

A journal can be a place to work out feelings and wrestle through problems. "It's a place for subjects I don't really want to talk to anyone else about," said one woman. It's a private place to record your relationship with God.

One friend told me this, which made me grin!

> My journaling time is definitely part of my quiet time with God. I can pour out my heart to Him. I can rant and rave to Him. I can write pages and pages and pages at a time or one line sentences like my favorite, "It's Monday and I'm still fat" entry from a few months ago. :) I write about changes I want to make in myself, in my life. I confess my sins, ask for forgiveness, and let him speak to me through it.

Such a practice reminds me of these words from Psalm 142: "I pour out my complaint before him; before him I tell my trouble" (v. 2). Sometimes we need to get things out in the open and work our way through them. At times I can't quite put words to things—and don't want to complain to Toben. But pouring out things to God helps me find the words, gives me perspective and insight.

Finding a practice takes . . . well, practice. I've heard more than
once that it typically takes at least thirty days to make something a
habit, so give yourself some time to settle into your practice.

I asked my friend Janna how she began her quiet time practice, and here's what she said:

> It was a very gradual process, but the first step was just
> making it a priority to get up earlier and just doing it.
> It meant going to bed a little earlier, setting the coffee
> maker, and putting out my books the night before
> right where I needed them. It took about two weeks
> for it to feel like my normal routine. But it did start
> coming naturally even after just a couple of days. By
> the end of two weeks, I even felt like I couldn't live
> without it!
>
> I started with a small amount of time at first—just
> doing my Bible study homework on weekdays, but by
> the end of that first month, I was doing my Bible study
> homework, praying, using my prayer book, and wor-
> shipping with music. Suddenly, an hour didn't seem
> like enough time!
>
> The time I spent in the mornings had such an ef-
> fect on my daily life that I was even sneaking in quiet
> time in preparation for worship service on Sunday.
>
> I've found that my prayer time is really what
> makes me feel close to God—praising him, worship-
> ping him, talking with him about everything. Days
> that I miss prayer, I feel scattered, misaligned, and
> usually a little out of control and dissatisfied by eve-
> ning. I've found that it's important for me to do my
> quiet time first thing in the morning, to ask God to
> order my day and establish the work of my hands like
> it says in Psalm 90.
>
> These days, being pregnant and having a two-
> year-old, I'm not getting up as early as I used to. For a
> while I felt frustrated because I wasn't getting "all my
> quiet time stuff" in. But it is only a season. And I've
> come to understand that sometimes "first thing" is just

sitting next to my daughter at the kitchen table for my quiet time while she eats breakfast, or it may mean 10 o'clock as I lay on the couch and pray out loud while Anne plays or colors in her "Bible study" book. I know God knows my heart and that my heart wants to be where he is.

The only thing is just to "stay the course." Sometimes if I'm out of the routine for a couple of days it seems like it's so hard to get back into it. But it's never hard at all if I actually just sit down and open his Word or start to pray. Then I wonder, "Why did I put this off?" Plus, after two days of not getting fed through my quiet time, my attitude, actions, and emotions all reflect it.

I remember Beth Moore saying that one request God will always say "yes" to is the request for more love for him and more love for his Word. I have found this so true and so important when I was starting out.

I remember laying in bed the night before starting this whole process and praying, "Lord, give me more love for you and your Word, and get me up in the morning refreshed, and get me OUT of bed." And he did! My advice is to ask him for a greater love for him and his Word and he will answer.

Though the particulars of my practice change from time to time, some things never change. Like Janna's, my time with the Father pretty much always includes time in the Word and prayer.

The Word of God

The primary way God speaks to us is through the Word. God is a God who communicates with his people. Jesus himself is called the Word in John 1. Coincidence? I don't think so. Communication is very important to God.

I'm so glad that God speaks to us, his people. Can you imagine how awful it would be if he didn't? If we didn't have the Bible, we'd simply have to guess and wonder what he thinks, what he requires of us. How uncertain and insecure I'd feel if I couldn't sing with confidence, "Jesus loves me! This I know, for the Bible tells me so."

God speaks to his people. Not so much through burning bushes or dreams these days, but through the written word—the Word of God.

Quiet time is the perfect time to sit still and read God's Word. Your Bible is more than just a book—it's "living and active" (Heb. 4:12). It has the power to be new and fresh with each reading.

Have you ever read a verse countless times, and then one time you read it, and it jumps off the page at you? Somehow that verse you've passed by fifteen times before suddenly speaks directly to you—to whatever you may be facing—with a fresh insight, a fresh meaning, a fresh voice. That's because the Word is alive.

This living Word is the breath of God—"God-breathed and is useful for teaching, rebuking, correcting and training in righteousness, so that the [woman] of God may be thoroughly equipped for every good work" (2 Tim. 3:16–17).

That astounds me. This book is able to teach me the most important things I need to know, to correct me when I'm wrong, to train me in righteousness. Through its power I am not just equipped—but *thoroughly* equipped for every good work. I want to know that book!

I love the Word—and especially my own well-worn copy. Do you have a Bible you love? If not, go get one! Bibles come in all shapes and sizes and colors. Find one that you love to hold, you love to carry, you love to open and read. I use the *NIV Study Bible*—it's full of helpful notes, has a good concordance, great maps and charts.

King David loved the Word of God, too, and he didn't even have the whole thing that we have today. For him, the Word was the Pentateuch, the first five books of the Old Testament—Genesis, Exodus, Leviticus, Numbers, and Deuteronomy. Imagine what he would think of the Gospels, or Isaiah, or Philippians. I'm certain his poet's heart would thrill to Philippians 2 or 1 Corinthians 13.

Just look at what David said in Psalm 119 about the Word of God. Go . . . grab your Bible and take ten minutes or so to read through it, noting how many times he refers to God's Word, God's law, God's precepts.

Ready? The entire psalm just gushes—there's really no other word for it—about how much David loves God's Word. Take a look at some of the things he says about it:

- It is to be fully obeyed (v. 4).
- Living according to God's Word keeps us pure (v. 9).
- When we hide God's Word in our hearts it keeps us from sin (v. 11).
- We can rejoice in keeping God's statutes (v. 14).
- God can open our eyes to see wonderful things in his law (v. 18).
- We can delight in God's statutes and go to the Word for counsel (v. 24).
- We find strength in the Word of God (v. 28).
- God shows us grace through his law (v. 29).
- God's Word preserves our lives (v. 37).
- We can trust in God's Word (v. 42).
- We can put our hope in God's law (v. 43).
- We find freedom when we seek God's precepts (v. 45).
- We find comfort in God's law (v. 52).
- We practice obedience to God's precepts (v. 56).
- Following God's precepts is a basis for friendship with others (v. 63).
- We can believe in God's commands (v. 66).
- God's law is precious—worth more than "thousands of pieces of silver and gold" (v. 72).
- God's Word is eternal and stands firm (v. 89).
- God's law sustains us in affliction (v. 92).
- God's commands make us wiser than our enemies (v. 98).
- God himself teaches us his law (v. 102).
- God's Word is sweet to the taste (v. 103).
- God's precepts give us understanding (v. 104).
- God's Word is a lamp and a light, showing us the way to go (v. 105).
- God's Word is awesome (v. 120).
- God's statutes are wonderful (v. 129).
- God's law is true (v. 142).
- God's statutes will last forever (v. 152).

- God's law gives us peace and protects us from stumbling (v. 165).

Wow! I feel a little out of breath! I want to love God's Word like this, don't you? To feel such passion and fervor for God's instruction.

So how do we develop a similar love for God's Word? Ask him. How else? Read it. Seems pretty simple, but the more time we spend reading the Word, the more we love it. That's just the way it works.

I'm all for reading other great books that teach me about God. But I need God's Word to *me*. So my quiet time is spent studying his Word. I want to see with my own eyes, hear with my own ears how God speaks to me through his Word.

Sometimes it can take awhile to develop an appetite for something new. As my kids will tell you, it takes something like eight or ten times of trying a new food before you really know if you like it or not. (Of course, they'll tell you this because I tell them all the time. Brussels sprouts . . . again?)

If you start reading the Word and find yourself bored, or just not getting it, or not sure about the whole thing . . . don't give up! Give yourself time to develop an appetite for the Word. Ask God to give you a greater appetite for it. We can be sure it's one prayer that he loves to answer with a resounding "Yes!"

Need some extra incentive? Take a look at Psalm 19:7–8, and read what else David wrote about the Word of God. Just as in Psalm 119, he uses words like *law, statutes, precepts,* and *commands.*

> The law of the LORD is perfect,
>   reviving the soul.
> The statutes of the LORD are trustworthy,
>   making wise the simple.
> The precepts of the LORD are right,
>   giving joy to the heart.
> The commands of the LORD are radiant,
>   giving light to the eyes.

Did you catch that? God's Word *revives* you, it makes you *wise,* it gives *joy* to your heart, and it gives *light* to your eyes. Those are all things I want—things I need—each and every day.

David goes on to say that "[God's ordinances] are more precious than gold, than much pure gold; they are sweeter than honey, than honey from the comb" (v. 10). Ask God to make it so for you.

He then says that "in keeping [God's ordinances] there is great reward" (v. 11). What kind of a reward? God himself. As he told Abraham in Genesis 15:1, "I am your shield, your very great reward." We find God in the pages of Scripture. That's the kind of reward I want.

Writing in the Word

If you don't already, write in your Bible. It's yours—not a library book—and I promise you won't get into trouble. I love what Beth Moore has said on more than one occasion: "God wrote it to you; write back!" Jot down your thoughts in the margins, add notes to remind you of a fresh insight into a favorite Scripture, note names and dates when you pray Scripture for others.

Why? For one, it helps you remember things when all your senses are involved. See it on the page, speak it aloud, hear your voice say the Word of God, write down what he's teaching you.

The other reason I write in my Bible is so I can go back and thank God for the work he does in my life. One morning at Bible study we were told to turn to Psalm 77:13–14, which says, "Your ways, O God, are holy. What god is so great as our God? You are the God who performs miracles; you display your power among the peoples."

Next to the verse I'd written in the margin, "For Toben, 3/04." At that time he was struggling after being diagnosed as bipolar, our marriage was struggling through the difficulties that go with such a disease, our family was struggling to stay together. I felt hopeless, and we desperately needed a miracle—a display of God's power in our lives. I begged God to display his power in our family.

That morning in Bible study it was March again—exactly one year later. I remembered writing that note as I prayed for Toben a year earlier, but I more clearly remembered that God had, indeed, answered my prayer.

I couldn't keep quiet and told my Bible study group about

it. They had prayed so faithfully for us and I wanted them to see God's faithfulness too. "You have to see how God has worked in our marriage!" Not only was I able to praise God, but they praised God with me.

And there's another note in the margin now: "How God has kept his promise! 3/05."

My Bible is filled with notes—from sermons, from Bible study lessons, from my own quiet times with God. Those notes help me grab hold of what God is teaching, to cement such lessons in my heart and mind as I see them again and again.

Each time I open my Bible, I see reminders of God's faithfulness to me, to our family. He is good—without a doubt, and I have written evidence!

A quiet time journal of some sort would be another way to record God's faithfulness and all he has taught you. How precious to go back through them and see how God taught you things just when you needed to know them.

One woman told me, "I do keep a journal. Actually, I write out my prayers. It keeps me from falling asleep, particularly now that I'm an early riser! I've been doing this for about ten years, on and off. I find that when I do journal, I'm much more focused on how I am growing in the Lord. I go back and read them periodically to remind myself how I felt about certain situations and how faithful God was in supplying my needs."

"His Word My Hope Secures"

We sang "Amazing Grace" in church the other Sunday. We sang almost all the verses, including the fourth verse:

> The Lord has promised good to me,
> His Word my hope secures;
> He will my Shield and Portion be,
> As long as life endures.[1]

I love the line that says, "His Word my hope secures." Our hope is in God, and his Word secures that hope—ties it down to something tangible and specific. In his Word we see God's character demonstrated, his mercy and grace at work.

Look at what the verb *secure* means: "to get hold or possession of; procure; obtain . . . to free from danger or harm; make safe . . . to effect; make certain of; ensure . . . to make firm or fast, as by attaching . . . to lock or fasten against intruders . . . to protect from attack by taking cover, by building fortifications, etc."[2] Synonyms for *secure* include "protected, stable, fast, fixed, confident, protect, guard, safeguard, assure, guarantee."[3]

We literally attach our hope in God's Word. It is the anchor that makes our hope firm. God's Word protects our hope from attack; it makes our hope stable, confident. It guards and guarantees our hope.

What does this kind of protection look like in everyday life?

We can secure our hope in God, for instance, as we wait for an anticipated phone call, for we read in the Word that the woman who fears the Lord will "never be shaken . . . [she] will have no fear of bad news; [her] heart is steadfast, trusting in the Lord. [Her] heart is secure, [she] will have no fear" (Ps. 112:6–8).

When overwhelmed by past sin, and we doubt that we've been fully forgiven, we hope that God has, indeed, forgiven us. We secure that hope, tie it down to something specific in the Word as we read, "O Israel, put your hope in the Lord, for with the Lord is unfailing love and with him is full redemption" (Ps. 130:7).

We look again to Scripture and read, "Who is a God like you, who pardons sin and forgives the transgression of the remnant of his inheritance? You do not stay angry forever but delight to show mercy. You will again have compassion on us; you will tread our sins underfoot and hurl all our iniquities into the depths of the sea" (Mic. 7:18–19).

Our hope is secure because God has said what he will do. And he always keeps his word.

Whenever we step out into a new direction at God's prompting, we are often fearful. But we secure our hope—we place our confidence—on the assurance of Scripture that our competence comes from God (see 2 Cor. 3:5–6). Thus, we can do "everything through him who gives me strength" (Phil. 4:13).

We pin our hope in God to Scripture. The Word is the guarantee that our hope is well-placed.

Know the Word

Spending time in the Word, learning what it says, is critical. And there is an important reason. We *must* know what it says.

Recall that the first time we encounter Satan in Scripture, he's in the garden, planting seeds of doubt in Eve. The first words recorded from his mouth are, "Did God really say . . . ?" (Gen. 3:1).

I've heard it said that Satan is not very creative. Throughout history, and today, he uses the same old tricks. And when he comes sowing seeds of doubt, he often still begins with that same old line, "Did God really say . . . ?"

We must know what God's Word says. There's no other way to put it. We must know what it says so we can answer with confidence when the Devil comes calling.

In Ephesians 6:17, in the passage that exhorts us to put on the full armor of God, Paul calls God's Word the sword of the Spirit. With this sword—with the Word of God—we can do battle with the enemy and send him scurrying back to hell. The Word, that book sitting on your coffee table, is a powerful weapon. But to use it, we must know what it says.

And to know what it says, we must study it—beyond sitting through a service on Sunday morning. I love this quote by Henrietta Mears:

> We are all busy and must take time for [reading the Bible]. If we are going to know the Bible, we must give time to it and arrange for it. We must adjust our lives so that time is made. Unless we do, we shall never come into any worthy knowledge of the Word; for it is impossible from pulpit ministry to acquire that needful knowledge of the Word.[4]

"We must adjust our lives so that time is made." It takes time to "come into any worthy knowledge of the Word." If we're going to know the Word—really know what it says and what it means and how it applies to our lives today—we have to give time to it.

You're on the right track, pursuing quiet time and making time in the Word a priority. Time is a precious commodity, and using it to know the Word is a valuable way to spend it.

You may be thinking, *Oh no, this is starting to sound like school.* Maybe you're feeling this is a bit like studying for a chemistry test. *Do I have to?*

I don't know about you, but I love being a student. When the end of summer rolls around and we head out to buy school supplies, I always feel a little jealous of my girls. I want new pencils, too. And some fresh pads of paper. And some pretty folders. So in addition to picking up the items on their lists, I usually buy myself some new things—paperclips and index cards, pens and crayons. I'm a bit strange, perhaps, but that's just how I am.

I think learning is fun. I tell Audrey and Emma all the time that I pray they'll love to learn, that they'll never stop learning—even when school is long done. I point out the new things I'm learning—whether it's some craft like a new embroidery stitch, something culinary like a new recipe, or something silly like a new song for Girl Scouts.

Whether you're a natural student or not, studying God's Word is exciting. Nothing is in there by accident and it all fits together perfectly—just waiting for us to see how each part illuminates the others, how even our story fits into the story of God's love for the world.

Here's something else about knowing the Word. God uses people who know the Word to influence the lives of others. When a friend is struggling, isn't it wonderful to point her to Scripture, to speak the truth, and encourage her with the Word rather than just an opinion?

Take a look at 1 Peter 3:15: "Always be prepared to give an answer to everyone who asks you to give the reason for the hope that you have." And Colossians 4:6: "Let your conversation be always full of grace, seasoned with salt, so that you may know how to answer everyone."

How is that possible? By knowing the Word.

Study the Word

How do we study the Word?

Henrietta Mears was an amazing woman, passionate about the Word of God. She built one of the largest Sunday schools in the world while serving as the Christian education director at First Presbyterian Church of Hollywood from 1918–1963. The curriculum that she wrote for her Sunday school classes was so popular that she founded Gospel Light Publications in order to publish it and make it available to all who requested it. She was also the founder of Forest Home—a Christian conference center in California—where my family visited often when I was small.

Here's what she had to say about studying the Bible:

> In one sense we should treat the Bible as we treat any other book. When we get a book from the library we would never treat it as we do the Bible. We would never think of reading just a paragraph, taking some ten minutes, reading a little at night and then reading a little in the morning, and so spending weeks, perhaps months, in reading through the book. . . .
>
> Read a book a week. Now don't suppose that this is impossible. It is not. How much time do you spend reading in 24 hours? How much time on newspapers? magazines? How much time do you give to fiction? to other reading? And how much time do you give to television? Now the longest of these books doesn't take longer than some of you devote to reading or watching television in one day.[5]

Start by reading it. Get familiar with it and learn where things are found—who wrote what books, what each book is about.

Mears's book, *What the Bible Is All About*, is a great place to start. You'll find helpful commentary, information on the styles of writing found in Scripture, summaries of each book of the Bible, background on those who wrote Scripture, reading plans, and more. (Some other helpful resources are included at the back of this book.)

Study a Book of the Bible

Ready for more in-depth study? Pick a book of the Bible and study it. Buy or borrow a commentary that will give you more information. Use the notes in your Bible and check the cross-references. (If your Bible has these features, it will also have instruction for how to use them.)

Keep a journal along with your Bible. After reading the whole book, go back and read it a few verses at a time. Write down what the verse is saying in your own words. Make some notes about how it applies to you specifically. Ask questions about things you don't understand. Turn the verses into prayer.

This is called inductive Bible study, and you can do it. Start with a short book—Philippians, for example—and give yourself however long it takes to finish.

Here's an example of what that might look like from Philippians 1:9–11:

Philippians 1:9–11
And this is my prayer: that your love may abound more and more in knowledge and depth of insight, so that you may be able to discern what is best and may be pure and blameless until the day of Christ, filled with the fruit of righteousness that comes through Jesus Christ—to the glory and praise of God.

Notes:
- Love increases with knowledge and insight.
- It takes discernment to know what is best.
- As love abounds, so does purity.
- I can be filled with the fruit of righteousness.
- Righteousness comes through Jesus Christ.
- God is glorified when I'm filled with fruit, when I discern what is best, when my love abounds.

Questions:
- How does love abound? Paul prays for it. I can pray for this too.
- What is the day of Christ? Look up in concordance.
- What does the fruit of righteousness look like? Is this like the fruit of the Spirit found in Galatians 5:22?
- In what areas of my life do I need to discern what

is best? What decisions am I facing that require discernment?

Prayer:
O God,

I want my love to abound more and more like this verse says. I want to love my family like this—more and more each day.

I want to discern what is best. Please show me the way you would have me go. Especially as I parent the girls—help me know what is best for them and for our family.

I want to bring you glory and praise. Please fill me with your Spirit today that I may bear much fruit—love and joy, peace and patience, kindness, goodness, faithfulness, gentleness, and self-control.

I pray this for Audrey and Emma too, Lord Jesus. I pray that their love for one another may abound more and more. That you would fill them with knowledge—that they would love to learn about you. Give them discernment as they go through their days at school, interacting with their friends and teachers.

In the name of Jesus, whose day is coming soon, Amen.

Study a Particular Word or Idea in the Bible

Another way to study Scripture is to focus on a word or idea. You'll definitely need a concordance for this one. (A terrific online tool is listed in the Resource section at the back of this book.)

Look up the verses where a word is mentioned and note them in a journal. What does each verse say about that idea? How does your understanding grow with each new verse?

You might also want to find a good Greek or Hebrew lexicon to give you insight into the original meanings of words. Because the Bible was translated into English from other languages, it's helpful to look at different translations to see what new insights they may offer. (Again, the online resources listed at the back allow you to look up verses in different translations.)

I like to study from my *NIV Study Bible*, but I love the insight I get when reading another translation or paraphrase. The Amplified Bible and *The Message* are two other versions that I enjoy using for study.

Last summer, I did a word study on *humility*. That topic kept popping up in the months leading up to summer. Without Bible study homework or kids to get to school, summer was an ideal time to pursue a word study on my own.

There's really no right or wrong way to do this kind of study. I just started and went where it led:

I looked up the word *humility* in the dictionary and noted the definition. I also looked up any synonyms for *humility*.

I used an online tool to search Scripture for words like *humility* and *humble*. I printed them out and read through them, making notes to myself about what the Bible says about being humble.

I checked other versions of the Bible to see where else *humble* or *humility* might show up.

I wrote any key verses on index cards, keeping them handy so I could reflect on them throughout the day.

I got really brave and looked up the original Greek and Hebrew words for *humility*. I noted their definitions and found where they were used.

And I noticed that Moses was commended for his humility: "Now Moses was a very humble man, more humble than anyone else on the face of the earth" (Num. 12:3). So I decided to take a closer look at him, which leads to another way to study Scripture.

Study a Person in the Bible

Does one particular biblical figure grab your interest, make your imagination soar? Maybe there's more than one.

Read about those people in your Bible. Find where their stories are told. Make a timeline for their lives. Note the things that stand out to you about their characters, about the choices they made. How did they seek God? What can you learn from their lives?

Commentaries will help with this kind of study, as well as books that have been written about these people. Many books have been written about the lives of Bible greats like Paul, David, and Moses; Mary, Ruth, and Esther.

Again, keep a journal, noting what you find. In the future, those journals from your Bible study become great references, tools to use as you grow.

There are all kinds of ways to study the Bible. Pick one that intrigues you and go for it! Ask other women what they're studying, how they've studied God's Word. Maybe ask a friend to do a similar study with you and meet together to share what you've learned.

I'm a huge fan of organized Bible study as well. Find a Bible study group at your church or in your neighborhood, and get involved. Doing your Bible study homework can be a great way to spend your quiet time in the Word.

R.S.V.P.

Ready for some new school supplies? Pens, pencils, high-lighters, a new notebook, and maybe some index cards for good measure.

Are you ready to study the Word? How are you going to begin? Pick a study method and get going!

- Study a book of the Bible.
- Do a word study.
- Pick a person in the Bible and learn from her or him.

Do you need anything to start your study? Commentaries, a computer hooked up to the Internet? Don't have what you need? Ask friends at church if you can borrow an item, or check out the church library and see what it has to offer. And don't forget the local library, too.

Gather your supplies and get ready—don't forget to set them out the night before!

Wait! you may be thinking. *You mentioned prayer as part of a quiet time practice.* You're right! The next chapter talks about the practice of quiet-time prayer.

CHAPTER 5

Finding Prayer

O what peace we often forfeit,
O what needless pain we bear,
All because we do not carry
Everything to God in prayer.

Prayer is simply conversation with God. Doesn't sound too complicated, right? Yet many of us struggle with prayer as we wonder how to do it, when to do it, what to say, what not to say.

If we're honest, talking is not something we struggle with. Just ask my husband—he knows I'm a champion when it comes to talking to my friends. We just bought a new phone for the kitchen, and it has a timer telling us how long we've talked when we hang up. I'm amazed that a quick call to a friend I've just seen, and will see again tomorrow, can take forty-seven minutes and twelve seconds. I just called to ask her one quick question. Honest!

Can you relate? Are you a Chatty Cathy like me?

So why are many of us tongue-tied when it comes to talking to God?

I love listening to my kids say their prayers at night. They've never been ones for "Now I lay me down to sleep . . ." They've always just prayed whatever is on their minds.

"Dear Jesus, I fell down at school today and it really hurt."

"Dear Jesus, I really love my dad."

"Dear Jesus, please help me to have good dreams tonight."

While they do from time to time ask for things apart from sweet dreams, they mostly just tell God what's on their minds and thank him for things. It's easy and natural, nothing forced or awkward. They just talk to Jesus like he's their BFF.

Maybe this is why Jesus told us that we must be like little children.

Easy, natural prayer can take time to develop. But ask God to help and he will! Ask him to turn your thoughts toward him, to teach you what it means to pray without ceasing, so that your walking around, moving-through-your-day thoughts naturally develop into a conversation with him.

Lord, Teach Us to Pray

We're not the only ones who have wondered how to pray. Take a look at Luke 11:1: "One day Jesus was praying in a certain place. When he finished, one of his disciples said to him, 'Lord, teach us to pray.'"

Can't you just see it? Jesus in prayer, perhaps on his knees, perhaps on his face, pouring out his heart and soul to the Father. Maybe he prays aloud, maybe only his lips move. The disciples gather around, keeping their distance, not wanting to intrude, but curious as to what Jesus is saying. They nudge one another, "What's he saying?" asks one. "I've never seen anyone pray like that before," comments another. "Could we pray like that?" whispers yet another. Something must have spurred their interest.

Which one, do you suppose, was bold enough to ask the question? "Lord . . . Master . . . Jesus . . . would you teach us how to pray like you pray?"

The prayer that Jesus taught them is known as the Lord's Prayer—the one many of us know by heart. In fact, it's part of the morning office in the prayer book I use each day, and it's all too easy to rattle it off by rote because of its familiarity.

But this is how Jesus responded to the disciples' question. And as I long to learn to pray as Jesus did, the Lord's Prayer is worth examining in greater detail.

Here's what Jesus told them as recorded in the gospel of Matthew:

> Our Father in heaven,
> hallowed be your name,
> your kingdom come,
> your will be done
> on earth as it is in heaven.
> Give us today our daily bread.
> Forgive us our debts, as we also have
>   forgiven our debtors.
> And lead us not into temptation,
> but deliver us from the evil one.
>   Matthew 6:9–13

When I slow down, pondering anew each phrase of this prayer, it directs my thinking, and teaches me to pray more effectively. Let me explain.

Our Father in Heaven

Right off the bat, this phrase gives me food for thought. Something about it calls to mind God's vastness, his infinite glory, his sovereign control over all things. I'm reminded of how small I am, and amazed that, despite God's presence in the heavens, he is also here with me—Immanuel, God with us. My Father, who knows each star by name, also knows my name and the details of my life. I stop and praise him for who he is—El Elyon, God Most High, the one true God.

Hallowed Be Your Name

God calls me by name, and I can call him by name, too. Do you know some of the names for God? I've mentioned before Ann Spangler's book, *Praying the Names of God*, and recommend it if you want to learn more about the names of God revealed in the Word.[1] Look at just a few of the names of God found in Scripture:

- *Elohim:* God, Mighty Creator
- *El Roi:* The God Who Sees Me
- *El Shadday:* God Almighty
- *El Olam:* Eternal God
- *Adonay:* Lord, My Master

- *Yahweh Ish:* Lord, My Husband
- *Yahweh Shalom:* The Lord is Peace
- *Abba:* Father

Who do you need God to be for you today? Bless his name and tell him who he is to you. "I will exalt you, my God the King; I will praise your name for ever and ever" (Ps. 145:1).

This practice has become so meaningful to me in my prayer time. At different times, different names of God have been most dear to me. When Toben and I were struggling in our marriage, and I felt so alone, it meant the world to me that God is Yahweh Ish—Lord, my husband. I needed a husband to talk to, a husband to help with the children, a husband to cherish me. And God met that need through his identity found in that name.

As I write a book, God's name of Elohim is particularly important to me. He is God, Mighty Creator—and I look to him for creativity, for inspiration.

What do you need today? Do you need an Abba, a daddy to turn to for love and comfort? His lap is waiting for you—crawl up and snuggle under the protection of his strong arms.

Do you need peace in the midst of a storm? He is Yahweh Shalom—the Lord is Peace—and he offers you "peace that transcends all understanding" (Phil. 4:7).

Bless his name—and how it reveals his character and meets your needs.

Your Kingdom Come

I love these words from the book of Job: "In the end he will stand upon the earth. And after my skin has been destroyed, yet in my flesh I will see God; I myself will see him with my own eyes—I, and not another. How my heart yearns within me!" (19:25–27). And these from 1 Corinthians 15:51–52: "Listen, I tell you a mystery: We will not all sleep, but we will all be changed—in a flash, in the twinkling of an eye, at the last trumpet. For the trumpet will sound, the dead will be raised imperishable, and we will be changed."

Jesus is coming back to earth one day. Here. To this earth. His feet will touch the ground and he will call his people to him.

There are days when the weight of the world is oppressive. Days when all the news is bad news. Days when the groans of the whole creation seem audible to our ears (see Rom. 8:22). On those days especially, I cry out, "Your kingdom come!" and I echo the prayer of John at the end of the book of Revelation, "Amen. Come, Lord Jesus" (22:20).

Your Will Be Done on Earth as It Is in Heaven

God's will is a good thing. I think of Romans 12:2, which describes God's will as good, pleasing, and perfect.

Yet even knowing that God's will is good and perfect and "immeasurably more than all we ask or imagine" (Eph. 3:20), I have a will too—a strong one. Just ask my mother! (Does your mother ever tell you she hopes you have a child just like you? My mom did—and it happened. In fact, I have two of them!)

Like the apostle Paul, I struggle with doing what I do not want to do, and not doing what I want to do (see Rom. 7:15). It's just part of being human. Sin doesn't die easily—not without putting up a hard fight. And so, like Paul, we cry, "What a wretched man I am! Who will rescue me from this body of death?" (7:24).

Who will rescue? Jesus. He is my rescuer—and yours. "Thanks be to God—through Jesus Christ our Lord!" (7:25). As Paul wrote later in Philippians: "It is God who works in you to will and to act according to his good purpose" (2:13).

So my prayer is for God's will to be done here on earth—in me, in my family, in our school, in our church, in our town, in our state, in our nation—as perfectly as it is done in heaven. I pray for God to make his will my own—to change my stubborn desires, to set my mind on things above (see Col. 3:2).

I pray for him to change my desires, lest I become like the Israelites, and God gives me what I want, but sends a leanness to my soul.[2] Do you know what I mean? I don't want to be so strong willed, so stubborn that God gives me what my will demands—even if it's not the best thing for me.

Give Us Today Our Daily Bread

Oh how I love this prayer! Notice that it says "today" and "daily" in one small phrase. This idea of dailiness must be important. Why else would God repeat it in just six little words?

Following God is a daily thing. Jesus said we must take up our cross *daily* and follow him (see Luke 9:23). We see the idea all through Scripture.

For the children of Israel wandering the desert, manna came each day—and only enough for that particular day was to be gathered by the people. Moses had this to say about the purpose of manna:

> Remember how the LORD your God led you all the way in the desert these forty years, to humble you and to test you in order to know what was in your heart, whether or not you would keep his commands. He humbled you, causing you to hunger and then feeding you with manna, which neither you nor your fathers had known, to teach you that man does not live on bread alone but on every word that comes from the mouth of the LORD. (Deut. 8:2–3)

It's so interesting that manna gathered in excess didn't save for the next day. God commanded his people to gather just enough for each day—double only for the Sabbath. Manna was designed for each day in its turn.

There's a rhythm in this provision. We hunger for God, and he feeds us. Then we hunger anew, and he feeds us again.

We don't need to hoard God. To go to church on Sunday and then hope it will sustain us for the week. This book you're now reading is all about God's *daily* provision. God has a word to feed you for *today*. He will have a word to feed you for *tomorrow*. But your word for today only comes today. If you miss a day, you can't go back to yesterday and find what you missed. And you can't know what you'll need tomorrow.

Oh my dear sister, hear me on this. God wants to feed you— each and every day. He has spread a feast for you and is waiting to come and dine with you. Revelation 3:20 says, "Here I am! I stand at the door and knock. If anyone hears my voice and opens the door, I will come in and eat with him, and he with me."

Don't try to eat on the run. Don't just grab a bite here and there. Prepare yourself. Sit down at the table and enjoy the feast with him. Take your time and enjoy his company. "Taste and see that the Lord is good" (Ps. 34:8).

I was reminded of this just recently as I reread *The Voyage of the Dawn Treader*, the third book in the Chronicles of Narnia series by C. S. Lewis. The travelers come to Ramandu's country and find a banquet set and waiting.

> "Why is it called Aslan's Table?" asked Lucy presently.
> "It is set here by his bidding," said the girl, "for those who come so far." . . .
> "But how does the food keep?" asked the practical Eustace.
> "It is eaten, and renewed, every day," said the girl. "This you will see."[3]

The king has prepared a banquet for you today. You need—I need—the nourishment he has ready and waiting. Sit, dine, and watch it be renewed tomorrow.

Forgive Us Our Debts, as We Also Have Forgiven Our Debtors

One thing that I'm learning is the practice of confession. I'll just tell you up front—it's not fun. I don't particularly like it. But I'm coming to understand that confession is necessary for forgiveness.

In the Old Testament, the Israelites washed before they entered the Tent of Meeting. Exodus 40:32 says, "They washed whenever they entered the Tent of Meeting or approached the altar, as the Lord commanded Moses." Confession washes us clean in the blood of the Lamb as we prepare to meet with our holy God.

And look at this from Exodus 34:33–35:

> When Moses finished speaking to them, he put a veil over his face. But whenever he entered the Lord's presence to speak with him, he removed the veil until he came out. And when he came out and told the Israelites what he had been commanded, they saw that his face was radiant. Then Moses would put the veil back over his face until he went in to speak with the Lord.

As we strip off our pretense, our masks, and acknowledge our sin, we too unveil before God. In confession, we stand before God without covering. Isn't it wonderful that we can trust him in such a vulnerable state?

The Word tells us to confess our sins so we can be forgiven (see 1 John 1:9). And so I've prayed for God to make me more and more aware of my sin, to open my eyes to my "hidden faults" (Ps. 19:12).

I'd like to think that I'm a pretty good person and that I don't sin "big," but the truth is "nothing good lives in me, that is, in my sinful nature" (Rom. 7:18). I am a sinner, and my sin separates me from the holy God. For me to be reconciled to God requires a payment, and Jesus made that payment in order to offer salvation to me. It is only through the sacrifice of Jesus that I am saved.

Don't for a minute think that I'm some kind of holy girl— gladly and gallantly confessing my state of sin and my need. No, I duck my head and grimace, praying such things with much fear and trembling, yet trusting that my confession, God's response, and his forgiveness will be far less painful than having such sin "rule over me" (Ps. 19:13).

Each day I ask God to forgive me for my pride, my unkind thoughts and words toward others, for wrong attitudes. I ask him to give me a fresh start, to wash me clean, to empty me of sin so he can fill me with his Spirit and work through me that day.

The benefit is this: to know how much I've been forgiven makes me love him more. Jesus said of the sinful woman, "I tell you, her many sins have been forgiven—for she loved much. But he who has been forgiven little loves little" (Luke 7:47).

But there is also this: we will be forgiven as we have forgiven others. As I pray for forgiveness, I pray that knowing how much Jesus has forgiven me will prompt me to forgive others—completely, quickly, lovingly.

And Lead Us Not into Temptation

Temptation is part of life. I'm tempted. You're tempted. Jesus was tempted. This world offers all kinds of tempting alternatives that claim to satisfy our cravings, bring us happiness, and free us from responsibility.

I pray that God will open our eyes to see through the glitter of temptation to the emptiness that lies beyond. To flee when it shows up on the horizon.

Paul wrote to the church in Corinth,

> So, if you think you are standing firm, be careful that you don't fall! No temptation has seized you except what is common to man. And God is faithful; he will not let you be tempted beyond what you can bear. But when you are tempted, he will also provide a way out so that you can stand up under it. (1 Cor. 10:12–13)

We are never beyond being tempted. And thinking we are is one way to walk smack-dab into the middle of it. Jesus said we must be "shrewd as snakes and innocent as doves" (Matt. 10:16). In this world, we need to walk about with our eyes wide open, alert for the nearest exit sign—the closest way out when temptation shows up.

I keep thinking about an airline safety presentation. Before take-off, we're told to stop what we're doing and listen to the message we've all heard again and again. But it bears repeating, and it bears our attention: "In the event of an evacuation, emergency lighting will mark the path to the exit. Take a moment to locate the exit nearest you. In some cases, the nearest exit may be behind you."

All too often, no one bothers to look up and look for the exit. God has provided a way out of temptation—we must be open to looking for it.

The above verses from 1 Corinthians are words that you can pin your hope to, as we talked about in the last chapter. When you're tempted, grab hold of the promise found here and declare with confidence, "God is faithful. He won't tempt me beyond what I can bear, therefore I can bear this. And he will provide a way out. I'm asking God to open my eyes to see the exit."

But Deliver Us from the Evil One

Satan is real. He's not a cute little imp prancing around with a pitchfork. No, he's cunning and knows my weaknesses and seeks my destruction. And he knows your weaknesses and seeks your destruction, too. It's a chilling thought, isn't it?

Once again we're back to the power of the Word. God has equipped us with the sword of the Spirit—the Word of God—to "batter back at the gates of hell."[4] God will deliver us, and one way he does that is through the power of Scripture. Know your Bible. Memorize his Word to you. Ask God to hide his Word in your heart (see Ps. 119:11) to remind you of the verses you know, to put his word in your mouth (see Isa. 51:16) so you can withstand the enemy.

And never forget that we know the end of the story:

> Hallelujah!
> For our Lord God Almighty reigns.
> Let us rejoice and be glad and give him glory!
> (Rev. 19:6–7)

And we are free!

Learning to Listen

As part of the conversation of prayer, ask God to teach you to listen. One-sided conversations grow old quickly. Do you know people who talk only of themselves? Who, in two minutes flat no matter the conversation, make it all about them with no room for anyone else?

So how do we listen to God?

To begin, read your Bible. I love my personal Bible, the one that I use all the time, and pray it will be like the widow's jar of oil that never ran out (see 1 Kings 17). I want my Bible to last my whole life. As I've mentioned before, it's so marked up that I could never begin to transfer all my notes and thoughts to a new one.

As I open it, I pray that God will "open my eyes that I may see wonderful things in your law" (Ps. 119:18). I pray that God will help me *see* what he wants me to *hear*—even if it's a passage that has grown familiar and old. As we learned previously, God's Word is alive—and can speak fresh each time we open it.

I also pray that God will give me an attitude to listen. I don't want what I hear from him to go in one ear and out the other. No. Instead, let's pray with Isaiah:

> The Sovereign LORD has given me an instructed tongue, to know the word that sustains the weary. He wakens me morning by morning, wakens my ear to listen like one being taught. The Sovereign LORD has opened my ears, and I have not been rebellious; I have not drawn back. (Isa. 50:4–5)

How do we do this? How do we listen as one being taught?

First we have to pay attention. In a previous book I've pondered about how I listen to God:

> Am I listening with just one ear—hearing the sound of his voice, but not really paying much attention to the words themselves? Am I giving him my full attention, watching intently to pick up on every gesture, every change in tone? Am I listening responsively? Am I listening with the intent of obeying? Or am I listening because I should, but really thinking of something else? Have I stopped what I'm doing to focus on him alone? Am I charging ahead with what I think he's said, or am I asking questions to clarify so that I can understand fully?[5]

Listening "as one being taught" takes me back to school—especially listening to lectures in college. To be taught, I had to listen with my full attention, to take notes on what I was told, to jot questions in the margins to ask the professor later. I had my own set of marks and squiggles to draw my attention to certain things, to remind me of what had been said.

For me, then, an obvious way to listen to God is to write down what he's telling me. Writing down things helps me remember them. Have you ever tried to run through the grocery store without a list? I come home with items not on the list and usually forget the one or two things I really needed. During this past week, I went to Costco and to the grocery store without a list and managed to make it home without milk—both times!

Listening "as one being taught" also suggests that I need to keep my mouth shut. It's awfully hard to hear two voices at once—and my voice can so easily drown out the voice of another. To "be still and know that he is God" is hard work. To discipline myself to read slowly and quietly, to listen intently to what God is saying in the Word—it requires concentration, focus, full attention.

Do I pay attention when he teaches me—in our time alone together or as I sit under the teaching of others? Or do I fidget, look at the clock, think of other things?

Let's not be like the man James describes who "looks at his face in a mirror and, after looking at himself, goes away and immediately forgets what he looks like" (James 1:23–24). No! How foolish! And yet without careful discipline, such foolishness comes all too easily.

Let's instead "be quick to listen" (James 1:19), and quick to "do what it says" (James 1:22). Let's seek the blessing that comes when we listen and do what we're told—the woman who looks "intently into the perfect law that gives freedom, and continues to do this, not forgetting what [she] has heard, but doing it—[she] will be blessed in what [she] does" (James 1:25).

But how do we really hear God's voice? God doesn't speak to me with an audible voice, telling me, "Joanne, do this or that." No. Rather, the Spirit indwelling me draws things to the forefront of my mind, makes words almost leap off the page of my Bible.

Recognizing God's Voice

I have a few friends whose numbers don't show up on my caller ID for some reason. They say hello and dive right into the conversation as I think, *Who is this?* As the conversation goes on, it usually takes only a moment or two for me to recognize a voice, as an inflection stands out or the topic is established.

There are times, too, when we think we hear something and wonder, *Is this God speaking?* So how do we know if it's God's voice—or our own?

Beth Moore's blog talked about this very subject. She wrote,

I bet, like me, you have had times when you felt prompted by the Spirit to do something that turned out to be your imagination or an embarrassingly stupid misinterpretation. Or, worse yet, [a] big mistake. Like the time I told a friend whose loved one was in a coma that I felt God had told me He was about to take the loved one Home . . . and, coincidentally, no sooner had I shared the prophecy than she woke right up. She's still alive and well, many years later and will most certainly outlive me just to spite me. I'm laughing so hard I can hardly keep my laptop still. I don't know why. I guess because we're just so danged absurd sometimes, aren't we?

One of my favorite stories a funny and humble friend of mine told me was about the time she awakened to hear the Scripture reference Philippians 6:13 in her heart over and over. She described how it echoed louder and louder within her like she imagined the voice of God beckoning young Samuel from his bed. She rose to see what personal revelation God would have for her, His dear servant, in that surely profound passage, only to find that Philippians ended at the fourth chapter. We both laughed until we cried. I've never forgotten the point of that story and have tried since to keep an appropriate measure of tentativeness about what I felt God was revealing to me until it was confirmed or affirmed.

So, aren't we all taken aback by the wonder that we—stiff of neck and stuffed of ear—really did hear from God on occasion? Oh, the mercy and tenacity of God to make Himself heard amid the clamor and clang of our attention deficit culture and self-absorbed souls! And, oh, to love Him more![6]

Can you relate, too?

Jesus said that his sheep know his voice (see John 10:4, 27). So how do we know if it's his voice we're hearing? Or if it's something from someone else or our own selves?

Did you catch what Beth wrote at the end—"until it was confirmed or affirmed"? What God says is always true to his nature and true to his Word. So often, I rush on ahead without waiting to make sure I heard correctly.

My girls do it all the time. Barely do I start talking and they're off and running, without waiting for me to finish giving my instruction. They often have to stop, come back, and hear me say, "Listen to all of what I have to say, *then* go do it." Instructions sometimes turn out differently when we wait for the *whole* instruction to be given.

In the book of Acts, Luke brags on the Berean's noble character for this reason: "for they received the message with great eagerness *and examined the Scriptures every day to see if what Paul said was true*" (Acts 17:11, emphasis added). Too often, I only *receive* with great eagerness and go rushing off without examining Scripture to confirm and affirm what I've heard.

I've found that when God wants to teach me something specific, he uses all kinds of ways to get my attention. Not only does the lesson invade my thoughts and leap off the page of Scripture, the same idea comes up in seemingly random conversation, is echoed in books I read, movies I watch, or songs I hear.

God's instructions are important; we can wait and trust him to affirm them.

R.S.V.P.

We could follow all kinds of guides for prayer. There's the ACTS prayer—Adoration, Confession, Thanksgiving, Supplication. There's what I call the "Pouring Prayer" that I learned from Beth Moore—Pour out confessions and concerns, Pour in the Spirit, Pour forth fruit.[7] There's the Lord's Prayer we studied together earlier. And there's also just praying whatever is on your heart.

They're all great. Pick one and follow it for the next few days. See if having a guide to follow keeps you on track, prevents your mind from wandering off, helps you organize your thoughts and conversation with God.

As you listen to God, take note of *how* you're listening. What distracts you? What helps you pay close attention? Is there a particular posture that makes listening easier?

Think about keeping a journal in which you record what God is saying to you. Note any verses he brings to your mind and what they mean for you that day.

If you think he's leading you in a new direction, make note of that, too. Ask God to confirm his direction. As you go back through your journal, pay attention to those themes that reoccur, and praise him for what he's teaching you.

☙   ☙   ☙

So we've got a plan and are ready to make quiet time a reality. Then up pops something that gets in the way. What to do? The next chapter looks at finding perseverance.

CHAPTER 6

Finding Perseverance

You need to persevere so that when you have done the will
of God, you will receive what he has promised.
(Heb. 10:36)

My mother always says, "There are seasons in life." Time moves on, things change, what once worked so well no longer seems to be working. We live through seasons of relative calm, and seasons when nothing seems normal. And in the midst of changing seasons, it can be hard to maintain time with God.

Before you know it, days have gone by and you haven't spent time with God or even thought about praying. *I blew it!* you think.

It's easy to get discouraged and give in to that little voice in your head that tells you, *It was too good to last,* and *Really, you're just not cut out for a spiritually disciplined life.*

In short, the newness has worn off; you've fallen off the wagon; you ate the whole gallon of ice cream despite being on a diet. Now what?

Remember that old saying about getting right back on the horse? It's an old saying because it's true! Not that being true makes doing it any easier, of course. But it's true nonetheless.

Have you ever fallen off a horse? My sister once fell off a horse. She was about ten years old, and we were riding in a field. She was riding at a gallop across the field, and then her horse stopped—just like that. In slow motion, she flew over his head, somersaulted in the air, and landed in the dirt.

After making sure she was fine (she was, though a little bruised), our riding instructor gave her a leg up and put her right back up on that horse. I was horrified. I remember thinking how unfair it was, how wrong, how mean to make Kristen try it again. In my mind, she deserved some sympathy, a break from riding. But the instructor knew better.

Instead of giving in to defeat when we miss quiet time, we have to climb back up and try again. So you missed a few days, a week, a month. There's no time like the present to make a new beginning.

Perseverance

What is *perseverance* anyway? Here's what the dictionary has to say:

> . . . steady persistence in a course of action, a purpose, a state, etc., esp. in spite of difficulties, obstacles, or discouragement.[1]

And while we're being *swotty* (what we called being extra studious when I was in school in England), look at the synonyms for *perseverance*:

> . . . doggedness, steadfastness. Perseverance, persistence, tenacity, pertinacity imply resolute and unyielding holding on in following a course of action. Perseverance commonly suggests activity maintained in spite of difficulties or steadfast and long-continued application.[2]

There's that "in spite of difficulties" again.

Perseverance is part and parcel of making space for God. We follow a practice—a "course of action" with "purpose." This is just what we've been talking about together.

But in that definition, the phrase that jumps off the page at me is this: "in spite of difficulties, obstacles, or discouragement."

Often we do ourselves a disservice when we expect—or give

others the expectation—that being a Christian means life will be rosy from here on out. That following after Jesus is a walk in the park, filled with flowers and sunsets. Don't get me wrong—I do believe with my whole heart that Jesus is the answer to life's problems—but I don't think that he waves a magic wand to make those problems disappear. Yes, there are flowers and sunsets, but also weeds and sleepless nights.

Following God and making him first takes work. Following God each day, seeking him first in our lives, making space for him in days that are often filled with the unexpected—this is the stuff of perseverance. It takes perseverance, because at times part of life is difficulties, obstacles, and feeling discouraged.

In order to find perseverance, we have to face the obstacles.

What Gets in the Way?

Take another look at the definition of perseverance. It specifically pinpoints difficulties, obstacles, and discouragement.

Difficulties

What are the difficulties that get in the way of your quiet time? My difficulties that get in the way tend to be smaller things. Actually getting out of bed. Going to bed earlier the night before. Deciding what to do during quiet time. Stumbling blocks for sure, but not insurmountable.

While I tend to be a morning person in general, I have a hard time getting out of bed in the winter when it's cold and dark. I have a hard time getting out of bed when I know the coffee's not ready to go, or when there's a sink full of dirty dishes waiting for me downstairs.

For me, overcoming these kinds of difficulties isn't too hard—it just requires some action ahead of time on my part. I put the lights downstairs on timers so I come down to a lit room, rather than one that's pitch black. I get the coffee ready to go the night before so I can just push a button. I clean up the kitchen last thing before bed so I come down in the morning to order, rather than kitchen chaos.

What are some of the little difficulties that stand in the way of your quiet time with God? Can you do some things the night before that will make it easier to get out of bed with a good attitude the next morning? Make a list (here I go again!) of the things that make quiet time more challenging for you, and think about how you can alleviate those difficulties. If you get stuck, ask a friend for some creative advice.

The most frequent answer when I asked women about difficulties? "Kids, kids, kids!" Being interrupted and distracted by little ones (and big ones too!) needing something. The way so many women have overcome that difficulty is by getting up *before* their kids. Or by starting their day with the Father *after* the kids head off to school and the house is quiet once more.

As children get older, they can learn to recognize that quiet time is a special time for you and the Lord. Unless it's an emergency, they can wait to ask you questions. Set up a quiet time routine for them—a special picture Bible or story Bible they can read (or look at) while you read your Bible. Or a coloring book of Bible stories that comes out only during quiet time.

Obstacles

Obstacles are bigger in my mind than difficulties. Difficulties are like tree branches that have fallen in the road—you have to get out of the car and move them in order to proceed. Obstacles are more like an entire tree that falls across the road—no amount of muscle is going to move it so you can go on your way. An obstacle blocks your way forward.

Some of the obstacles in my life have been illnesses, crises, and life changes. Things that just take over life for a season and make concentrating on anything but the thing at hand next to impossible.

Some of these obstacles are good things—but obstacles nonetheless. Having a baby is a wonderful thing but it changes everything. Routines are up in the air, getting enough sleep becomes a new adventure each and every night, and each day is different as schedules accommodate a new life.

Other obstacles have been something as simple as a change of routine, a change of schedule that throws my daily practice out of kilter. Something as common as a weekend away has been an obstacle for me—my routine and environment change, and I have a hard time adjusting.

At times obstacles seem immovable, like a tree in the road. Other times, obstacles will go away in time, like a road that's just temporarily flooded.

So how do we deal with obstacles to quiet time?

Like Mom always says, life comes in seasons. Just the other day she and I were sitting around her kitchen table, talking about this, drinking tea while the girls played in her living room. There's always a season—it's not like one season comes to an end and that's just it. A new season always follows.

So in dealing with obstacles, first it helps me to remember my mother's wisdom. Life comes in seasons and "this too shall pass." I don't mean to sound trite or to discount whatever obstacle you may be facing. But, remember, it is a season and it will pass. Whatever you're dealing with today won't last forever.

And that's not to say that this season is always bad and the next is always good. Sometimes seasons are just different.

The second thing that helps is some rearranging. Just like that tree in the road requires a detour, obstacles sometimes require creative detour-like solutions. Like a change of routine, help from a friend or neighbor.

My friend Janna is getting ready to have her second baby. In fact, she's due in the next couple of weeks. Recently we were talking about our time with the Lord, and she's already anticipating the need to rearrange. She's not sure how it's going to look, but she knows it will be different. And that's okay. She may need to move her quiet time from morning to afternoon, at least until the baby has figured out a schedule of sorts, and Janna is more well-rested. She may need to spend time with the Father here and there, at odd moments throughout the day, rather than the big chunk of time she's used to now.

She's incredibly creative—and I have no doubt that she'll find an arrangement that will work.

Discouragement

In some ways, I think discouragement can be the biggest hindrance to quiet time. Overcoming discouragement can, in fact, require the most perseverance.

God, we pray, *I've been getting up, starting my day with you, and yet I don't see a difference. I thought that I'd somehow feel different, but I don't. I'm not sure of the point in continuing this practice.*

Make no mistake about it. Spending time with God will change you as you grow in intimacy with the Father, becoming more like him with each moment you spend together. That's part of God's plan. Unfortunately, it's not the kind of change that happens overnight.

And Satan has a plan for you, too. Never forget that he's a counterfeit—he's entirely unoriginal. If God wants to encourage you, Satan wants to *discourage* you—especially when it comes to knowing the Word of God.

The Word of God is your only offensive weapon in the armor of God. Make no mistake—war has been declared, and Satan is the enemy. If he can do anything to keep you from using that weapon, he will. Because if you're disarmed, you're not much of a threat.

Don't give in without a fight. Fight back!

When you're feeling discouraged in your quiet time, press in close to the Father with your disappointment. Don't turn from him or give up. Hide in the shelter of his wings (see Ps. 61:4), and let him be the lifter of your head (see Ps. 3:3).

Go to him and let him arm you for the battle.

When I'm feeling discouraged, I need encouragement. But instead of waiting for someone to come and encourage me, I can encourage myself through the Word—and so can you!

I'll never forget Beth Moore's saying this same thing as she stood on a platform in the center of the Pepsi Center in Denver. "David needed encouragement," she said. "And so he encouraged himself and spoke God's Word to his own heart." She dropped her head to her chest and mumbled into her collar, "'Why are you downcast, O my soul? Why so disturbed within me? Put your hope in God, for I will yet praise him, my Savior and my God'" (Ps. 42:5).[3]

We all laughed, but the image has stuck with me. I can speak my own encouragement from God's Word when I need it. Sure, I might feel a little silly, but it's my quiet time, and after all, God is the only one watching.

Which verses from Scripture encourage you the most? Write

them down, type them up on a bookmark for your Bible, keep a list handy and pull it out when you need encouragement to persevere.

Here are some of the verses that encourage me when I'm struggling to persevere in my quiet time:

> "No eye has seen, no ear has heard, no mind has conceived what God has prepared for those who love him"—but God has revealed it to us by his Spirit. (1 Cor. 2:9–10)

That makes me want to know what God has prepared for me.

> He wakens me morning by morning, wakens my ear to listen like one being taught. The Sovereign LORD has opened my ears, and I have not been rebellious; I have not drawn back. (Isa. 50:4–5)

God has something to teach me. How incredible is that? The Sovereign Lord of the universe who holds the world in his hand has something to teach *me!* That astounds me. It makes me want to wake up and pay attention and listen carefully.

> May our Lord Jesus Christ himself and God our Father, who loved us and by his grace gave us eternal encouragement and good hope, encourage your hearts and strengthen you in every good deed and word. (2 Thess. 2:16–17)

Not only will God give encouragement, he gives *eternal* encouragement. When I personalize this passage, it helps me to speak to my own heart: "Jesus loves me and God gives me eternal encouragement and good hope. He encourages my heart and he will strengthen me in every good deed and word." Say it over and over until it sinks in.

Keep Your Eyes on the Prize

The author of the book of Hebrews knew something about perseverance. He said,

> Therefore, since we are surrounded by such a great cloud of witnesses, let us throw off everything that hinders and the sin that so easily entangles, and let us run with perseverance the race marked out for us. Let us fix our eyes on Jesus, the author and perfecter of our faith, who for the joy set before him endured the cross, scorning its shame, and sat down at the right hand of the throne of God. Consider him who endured such opposition from sinful men, so that you will not grow weary and lose heart. (Heb. 12:1–3)

You and I, too, have a race marked out for us. One that requires perseverance. As we "throw off everything that hinders" us—the difficulties, obstacles, and discouragement—we must fix our eyes on the prize in order to endure the race ahead. There is joy set before us—the joy of intimacy with the Father as we are transformed day by day into the likeness of his beloved Son (see 2 Cor. 3:18).

To receive the prize, we need discipline. Here's what the apostle Paul said about running a race:

> Do you not know that in a race all the runners run, but only one gets the prize? Run in such a way as to get the prize. Everyone who competes in the games goes into strict training. They do it to get a crown that will not last; but we do it to get a crown that will last forever. Therefore I do not run like a man running aimlessly; I do not fight like a man beating the air. No, I beat my body and make it my slave so that after I have preached to others, I myself will not be disqualified for the prize. (1 Cor. 9:24–27)

I'm not a runner. (I can't breathe and run at the same time—and breathing is pretty important to me!) But I do know that running, that training for a race, takes discipline. It means getting up and running when you don't feel like it, heading out the door to run even when it's cold and rainy. It means trusting that the action of training will carry you through until the feeling of enjoyment returns.

Toben reminded me of the idea of muscle memory when we

were talking about this. "In a repetitive action like golf," he said, "after you hit thousands of golf balls, your body sort of remembers how to do it, even if you've taken a break." It's also true for hitting a tennis ball, riding a bike, throwing a baseball. Even if it's been a long time since you've practiced, once you know how to do it, it's easy to get back in the swing.

It's the same with quiet time. There will be mornings you won't want to get up, mornings when you'd rather stay in bed. Or mornings when you get out of bed but you'd rather turn on the television or pick up a novel than study the Word. Perseverance means trusting that the action—the discipline—of having quiet time anyway will carry you through until the feeling of wanting to returns.

When Toben and I were first married, I got some of the best advice I heard or read. I can't remember who said it, but the advice has stuck anyway. Here it is in a nutshell: There will be times when I won't *feel* loving toward Toben, but if I *act* loving anyway, then the feeling will follow.

The only way to test such advice is to follow Nike's advice— just do it. You won't know if it works until you try it.

In my relationship with Toben, when I act obedient, when I act in the way I know I should, my feelings do come around. And in persevering in my quiet time, when I get up anyway, when I open my Bible anyway, the feeling comes.

I don't mean to say that I pretend, that I fake it. That's not it at all. God knows when I'm struggling, so I just go ahead and tell him. "I'm distracted, Lord," I pray. "I'm tired and I don't really feel like doing this right now. But I'm coming to you anyway, and I ask you for a fresh word, a fresh insight. Restore the desire to meet with you."

I ask him to help me focus, to meet with me despite my unwilling heart. "I *want to* want to do this," I tell him. I pray that he'll guard me from distraction, keep my mind focused on him, increase my desire to press into him.

And though it may take a while, God always answers and rewards such perseverance.

The Parable of the Sower
The parable of the sower is a familiar one. It's the stuff of

Sunday school lessons for small children, told with the help of a flannel graph.

But as I was reading it the other day, something jumped off the page at me. You guessed it—perseverance. Maybe this parable is familiar to you, too. Take a minute and ask God to give you fresh eyes to see and ears to hear. Maybe read the following verses out loud, giving yourself a chance to hear them as well as see them on the page.

> While a large crowd was gathering and people were coming to Jesus from town after town, he told this parable: "A farmer went out to sow his seed. As he was scattering the seed, some fell along the path; it was trampled on, and the birds of the air ate it up. Some fell on rock, and when it came up, the plants withered because they had no moisture. Other seed fell among thorns, which grew up with it and choked the plants. Still other seed fell on good soil. It came up and yielded a crop, a hundred times more than was sown."
>
> When he said this, he called out, "He who has ears to hear, let him hear."
>
> His disciples asked him what this parable meant. He said, "The knowledge of the secrets of the kingdom of God has been given to you, but to others I speak in parables, so that, 'though seeing, they may not see; though hearing, they may not understand.'
>
> "This is the meaning of the parable: The seed is the word of God. Those along the path are the ones who hear, and then the devil comes and takes away the word from their hearts, so that they may not believe and be saved. Those on the rock are the ones who receive the word with joy when they hear it, but they have no root. They believe for a while, but in the time of testing they fall away. The seed that fell among thorns stands for those who hear, but as they go on their way they are choked by life's worries, riches and pleasures, and they do not mature. But the seed on good soil stands for those with a noble and good heart,

who hear the word, retain it, and *by persevering* produce a crop. (Luke 8:4–15, emphasis added)

Jesus explains the parable clearly.

The seed is God's Word. And the different kinds of soil—
the different places the seed lands—represent different kinds of
people. Those along the path hear the Word, and then the Devil
comes and steals it. Those on the rock hear the Word, receive the
Word, yet fall away when they face something that tests their faith.
Those among the thorns hear the Word, presumably receive the
Word, but do not mature because they are choked by life's worries.

Only the person represented by the good soil produces a
crop—the whole purpose of the seed. Why else does a farmer
plant seed but to produce a crop?

Every person represented in the parable of the sower *hears* the
Word of God. But, "It is not enough to hear the Word!"[4] All but
the one on the path *receive* the Word. But only the person who
hears the Word and retains the Word produces a crop. How? By
persevering.

Jesus said it is to his Father's glory that we bear much fruit
(John 15:8). That we produce an abundant crop. It is our calling—
Jesus said as much in John 15:16: "I chose you and appointed you
to go and bear fruit—fruit that will last."

We cannot do it without perseverance.

Our time with God—our hearing the Word that God sows
in our lives—must be received and retained. We must persevere
to think on it, to study it, even to commit his Word to memory
in order for it to take root in us and produce fruit for God's glory.
Simply put, we must do what it says. We must take the word that
we hear from God during our time with him, and then act on it.

James also has something to say that ties directly into Jesus'
parable of the sower: "Humbly accept the word planted in you,"
he writes in James 1:21. He goes on to say, "Do not merely listen
to the word, and so deceive yourselves. Do what it says" (v. 22).

The girls and I planted a small garden this past summer.
Nothing big, nothing too fancy. Zucchini, a tomato plant or two,
some carrots for the rabbits who live under our deck. Yet as small
as the garden was, it required some perseverance to produce a

crop. We battled against the weeds that threatened to choke the small plants. We watered every day to nourish the plants and safeguard them from the hot summer sun. We pruned and thinned out the carrots, giving them room to grow and thrive.

We learned together that tending a garden requires daily action. It wasn't enough to think about doing the chores associated with growing a garden. We had to put those thoughts into action. To just do it.

And so when I'm reading the parable of the sower and thinking, *I want to be the good soil*, I realize that it's going to require some daily perseverance.

Be Flexible and Ask for Help

I want to offer you some encouragement. Perseverance doesn't always mean doing things the same way you've always done them, world without end. Persevering doesn't mean getting up at 4:30 if it's not working.

You have to spend time with God in the midst of *your* life. And part of learning what will work for you is being flexible. If something within your quiet time just isn't working, try something new.

I'm not saying that if quiet time isn't working, give it up. Not at all! But within your quiet time practice, give yourself some flexibility. Just as great athletes cross train, you need some variety to persevere and grow. Or since we've established that I'm not an athlete, we can go back to the gardening analogy: just as plants need sun and rain and even cold to grow, we need variety too.

If you're bogged down in reading through Leviticus, supplement your reading with the Psalms or the Song of Solomon. If your prayers are getting stale and you're having trouble concentrating, try journaling your prayers for a while.

Sometimes I've found that perseverance can be as simple as switching the order of doing things during my quiet time. I usually pray first, but when I'm especially tired it can be hard to pray, and I get discouraged as my mind wanders and I yawn my way through the morning prayer. Doing my Bible study first—digging into the Word and seeing what God has revealed of himself there—is sometimes all it takes to wake me up and get me going.

In the midst of it all—difficulties, obstacles, discouragement—ask for help.

Talk to your girlfriends. Find out what's worked for them. Ask for practical help, too. Maybe some time together with those friends for encouragement. Some help with your kids so you can have some focused time to get back on track.

Ask God for his help, too. Romans 15:5 says that God gives "endurance and encouragement"—exactly what we need. The important thing is to give whatever you may be facing to God.

In talking about using a journal, the authors of *A Guide to Prayer for All God's People* admit there will be dry times: "At other times, you will write about dullness, your struggle to pray at all, discouragement. . . . Be entirely honest in your writing. Write for yourself and God alone!"[5]

Come to him with your need. Ask him for creativity to overcome difficulties. Ask him to remove obstacles or to show you the way over or around them. Ask him for his encouragement.

Ask him to produce a crop in you that will bring him much glory. Ask him to give you perseverance that "must finish its work so that you may be mature and complete, not lacking anything" as James writes (James 1:4). Pray the words of Philippians 1:6, that "he who began a good work in you will carry it on to completion until the day of Christ Jesus."

R.S.V.P.

Are you in need of some perseverance today? Sit down and identify the things that are getting in your way, being as specific as possible. What are you facing? Try organizing them by category so you can best know how to deal with them.

- Difficulties
- Obstacles
- Discouragement

As you think about each item on your list, is there an obvious solution you could pursue? If not, commit to praying about each one, asking God for his direction.

Make your own list of encouraging verses—the ones that lift

your spirits and give you renewed hope and faith. Write them on index cards and keep them close at hand—in your purse, in the car, at the kitchen sink.

Ask others for help, too. As you look at your list, are there ways others could help—your family, friends, community? Sometimes it can be hard to ask others for help. I have a hard time with it, too. But giving others an opportunity to help often allows them the opportunity to serve.

Sometimes it's as easy as asking friends about what's worked for them, what hasn't worked. Our girlfriends are often our best resources. They are who we ask when we want to find a new place to get a good haircut, when we need a great recipe for a company dinner, or when we need some parenting advice.

The advice I will give you is this: don't give up. I love this quote from John Wesley, founder of the Methodist movement: "O begin! Fix some part of every day for private exercises. . . . Whether you like it or no, read and pray daily. It is for your life; there is no other way: else you will be a trifler all your days."[6]

One last thing about perseverance—it's really a character quality. As we develop perseverance in our quiet times, it will affect other areas of our lives, too. Knowing that makes me want to persevere with perseverance—because I face difficulties and obstacles in other areas in my life. How about you?

🏺 🏺 🏺

One thing that fuels our perseverance is passion. The next chapter looks at developing passion for God.

CHAPTER 7

Finding Passion

Deliver us when we draw near to You,
from coldness of heart and wanderings of mind:
Grant that with steadfast thoughts and kindled affections,
we may worship You in spirit and in truth. Amen.
—A collect before worship

Do you have a passion for God? Part of persevering in daily time with God, in giving God first place in our lives, is developing passion for him. The kind of passion that inspired Psalm 42:1–2: "As the deer pants for streams of water, so my soul pants for you, O God. My soul thirsts for God, for the living God. When can I go and meet with God?" The kind of passion that caused David to write, "O God, you are my God, earnestly I seek you; my soul thirsts for you, my body longs for you, in a dry and weary land where there is no water" (Ps. 63:1).

How do we find passion like that?

Created in God's Passionate Image

"God created man in his own image, in the image of God he created him; male and female he created them" (Gen. 1:27). We are made in the image of a passionate God—one who feels deeply, loves extravagantly, and does things wholeheartedly.

As one made in God's image, what are you passionate about? Webster defines *passion* as "emotions as distinguished from reason;

intense, driving, or overmastering feeling or conviction; ardent affection; a strong liking or desire for or devotion to some activity, object, or concept."[1]

What moves you to tears or causes you to dance? To what do you give your entire focus, all your energy? For what do you work tirelessly, drop everything to pursue? What do you talk about, share with others, tell anyone who'll listen?

What's your passion?

All too often, my passion is directed at things that don't last, things that don't really matter. Time for true confession. I discovered a new store a couple of weeks ago and bought a new pair of jeans there. I blogged about them, told everyone who would listen about them, recommended this store to anyone who would listen.

Yes, they *are* great jeans—well made and oh-so-inexpensive. But they're just a pair of blue jeans, after all.

But when was the last time I told anyone about my Jesus—the one who reached down and pulled me out of bitterness and anger, the one who defines what passion really is? I want to pursue passion so I can pour out passion about Jesus to those around me. I want to be the most passionate about *him*.

The Passion of Christ

Here's something I found interesting. When I looked up *passion* in the dictionary, the very first definition was this: "the sufferings of Christ between the night of the Last Supper and his death."[2]

Why did Jesus consent to die, though he said, "My soul is overwhelmed with sorrow to the point of death" (Matt. 26:38)? Why did he submit to the Father, saying, "Yet not as I will, but as you will" (v. 39)? Why did the Father give up his only Son (see John 3:16)?

Why? Because of love. Passionate love for you. Passionate love for me.

Our passion for God is a response to *his* passion. When we stop and think of the passion he feels for his own—and we understand and believe that we are his own—how can we help but respond with passion?

In his book, *Reliving the Passion*, Walter Wangerin begins his preface with these words:

In the sincerest silence of my soul, I murmured over and over, "I love you, Lord Jesus."

Jesus was dying. I could do nothing to save him— not even to ease him. I could only watch and suffer the sorrow too. I was a child. Yet I saw every detail of his passion exactly as the Bible set it down. Everything. I learned everything. Not because I was precocious, but because I *felt* it all.

And always there came the moment when I burst into tears.

Jesus looked at me. The love in his face was so horrible that I started to cry, and I murmured over and over, "I love you, too! I love you, Lord Jesus."[3]

It was passionate love that inspired the passion of Christ. And when we see the love and the endurance and the determination behind his passion, we are moved to respond. To be loved greatly inspires great love in return.

When was the last time you stopped to think about the passion God has for you? Easter is an obvious time, as we remember the passion of Christ. Christmas is another, when we remember that God became a helpless baby in order to become Immanuel, God with us.

But the stories are often all too familiar, and we read the words quickly, without entering the story and feeling its emotion. We know the reason behind it, accept it willingly, but do not take the time to explore the "emotions as distinguished from reason" as Webster says.

Passion isn't reasonable. It's beyond reason, beyond logic, beyond understanding. It doesn't make sense that God would go to such great lengths to pursue his people, that he runs to welcome a prodigal, that Jesus . . .

> Who, being in very nature God,
>   did not consider equality with God
>   something to be grasped,
> but made himself nothing,
>   taking the very nature of a servant,
>   being made in human likeness.

> And being found in appearance as a man,
> he humbled himself
> and became obedient to death—
> even death on a cross!
> Philippians 2:6–8

It's beyond reason, beyond comprehension. It is *passion*.

Does it make sense that believers through the ages have stood up to persecution, torture, ridicule, death—for the sake of Christ? Read Hebrews 11 and try to make sense of it without passion.

> Others were tortured and refused to be released, so that they might gain a better resurrection. Some faced jeers and flogging, while still others were chained and put in prison. They were stoned; they were sawed in two; they were put to death by the sword. They went about in sheepskins and goatskins, destitute, persecuted and mistreated. (Heb. 11:35–37)

They were passionate because they embraced their identity as recipients of God's passion. With Paul, they would agree, "Whatever was to my profit I now consider loss for the sake of Christ" (Phil. 3:7)—Christ, who gave "his life as a ransom for many" (Mark 10:45).

Rescued and Forgiven

How do I know that God is passionate about me? How do I *feel* the emotion of his passion so I can respond in kind?

Two words come to mind—rescued and forgiven.

Rescued

When I stop to think how he has rescued me—from what he has rescued me—when I stop to remember how it felt before he rescued me—I'm undone, overcome with emotion and gratitude. Even as I sit here and write, tears are blurring my vision as I recall how God has proved his great love to me.

I was telling someone just the other day that I'm not the girl I used to be. And while I can't remember the exact moment I

changed—sometimes rescue isn't immediate, isn't defined with a dramatic moment in time—there's a definite before and after.
Here's what I recently wrote about it:

> I've been thinking a lot about poor Eustace [the dragon] after blogging about that quote from *The Voyage of the Dawn Treader* the other day. About the layers of his dragon-y skin being removed one at a time until he lets Aslan peel it all off right down to the core.
>
> And with that, I've been thinking about the whole pit thing (à la Psalm 40 and Beth Moore). There are definitely some pits in my past. Some pretty cavernous, others more like pot holes.
>
> But as I was doing my Bible study homework (*Jesus the One and Only*) yesterday morning, I came across this:
>
>> "Satan would rather return to a previous job on an individual than find a new one. Satan is a lot of things, but creative is not one of them. He ordinarily sticks to what has worked in the past . . . when he has attempted to return to an area in my life where he held a previous stronghold— even though he's already been forced to leave. Have you experienced something similar? Briefly explain."[4]
>
> Reading that, I had a little epiphany.
>
> My answer to Beth's questions was this: Yes! For me it's having a "thing"—an issue that crops up again and again. Those issues? Control, guarding my heart instead of letting God guard it, self-sufficiency.
>
> I answered the question and wrote in the margin about the things I struggle with, and I realized that they all stem from pride. Yuck. I've just been wandering around the edge for what seems like my whole adult life and falling in at different points around this huge, giant pit of pride.

Here's the story . . .

Control really cropped up for me once I had children. I've always been a well-ordered person and have liked to have my ducks in a row. Something I really don't think is bad. BUT . . . when my ducks revolt and run here, there, and everywhere, I couldn't handle it.

Anger—red-hot, uncontrollable, swallowing you in a huge gulp anger—was the result. I yelled at my kids, said horrible things, threw things around the house, lashed out at everyone and everything. It came on suddenly, taking me over, and made me feel even more out of control. I hated it, but couldn't stop. It was so unexpected, so frightening.

In the midst of all of this, my friend Hanna called me one day. "Joanne," she said, "control is an idol. You can worship control, or you can worship God." And then she hung up. (Do you have a friend like that, who speaks truth into your life unflinchingly? I hope so . . . because a friend like that is a wonderful gift.) It was the beginning of learning to give control to God each day. To see it clearly as something to hand over to him, to open my hands and not grab at control until my knuckles turned white with the effort.

It was a long process, years really. I still have to be on guard against control, but when it crops up now (like when the kids get sick in the middle of the night and my first reaction is anger because I'm so scared) I stop and think, "Oh, I know what this is and where it's coming from." I can say aloud, "Okay, God, I'm choosing to trust you in this, to let you be in control."

Guarding my heart was the next pit I fell into— well, jumped into willingly would be more accurate. When Toben was diagnosed as bipolar, life fell apart. In his pain and illness, he broke my heart—repeatedly. So I took it back from him. Literally. I told him one day, "I'll stick with you through this, but I'm taking my heart back. I don't trust you with it anymore."

And I told God the same thing. "You're not protecting my heart in this and it hurts too much. Your Word says that you'll guard my heart, but it doesn't feel like it, so I'm taking that job back."

Bitterness was the result. Choking, strangling bitterness. Have you ever heard that bitterness is like a weed? It's true. I could feel it strangling my heart, choking me. It may sound like I'm being overly dramatic, but that's exactly what it was. I could almost see it sending down roots and twisting around my heart.

I sat at a traffic light one morning—at the intersection of La Costa and El Camino Real—scarcely able to breathe. There have been times in my life when I've clearly heard the voice of God invade my thoughts. This was one of those times. "Guarding your heart is MY job, Joanne," he said. "Will you let me do it?" Tears rolled down my face and I let go and gave my heart back to those around me. It hurt like crazy, but slowly the grip of bitterness eased.

My heart still hurt, but it was a healthy kind of hurt—the hurt that comes from being real and alive, rather than the choking hurt bitterness afforded. And now when my heart gets hurt, I remember that it means I'm alive, and I'm free.

I'm slowly coming to see the pit for what it is— pride. Control was pride—thinking I could control things beyond myself. Guarding my heart was pride— thinking I could do God's job better than he could. And the latest pit I've been in is clearly pride as well.

Self-sufficiency is how pride has been manifesting itself lately. Thinking I don't need anyone and can do it all myself. Can't remember if I shared this definition of *humility* with you. It's from the book *TruFaced* and goes like this: Humility is trusting God and others with who I really am.[5]

Trusting God is easier for me than trusting others. God knows who I really am and there's no hiding from him. But trusting others is harder—especially those closest to me. Especially Toben, I think.

In the midst of his crisis, I learned to be self-sufficient out of necessity. Toben was so ill that he couldn't meet my needs. He needed all of his energy to turn to God, to heal, and become whole again. Self-sufficiency became a habit—one I became proud of, thinking I could get through anything—just me and God. But God created us for relationship—with himself and with others. And God created Toben and me for each other.

I am slowly giving up self-sufficiency. But no . . . that's not how it's done. I can't just think, *I got myself into this and I'll get myself out of it*. Because that's just more prideful self-sufficiency. Instead, I have to get down on my knees each morning, face to the carpet, and ask God to pull me out. To peel off the layers of my pride, like Aslan peeled skin from the dragon, and expose my need for him and for others. To give me a humble heart—"smooth and soft as a peeled switch and smaller than I had been." Because I want him to lead me to "the rock that is higher than I" (Ps. 61:2), to the place of peace and refuge that Eustace called "perfectly delicious."

> From Psalm 40:
> I waited patiently for the LORD:
> he turned to me and heard my cry.
> He lifted me out of the slimy pit, out of the
> mud and mire;
> he set my feet on a rock and gave me a firm
> place to stand.
> He put a new song in my mouth, a hymn of
> praise to our God.

Many will see and fear and put their trust in
   the LORD . . .
I desire to do your will, O my God;
your law is within my heart . . .
may your love and your truth always
   protect me . . .
Be pleased, O LORD, to save me;
O LORD, come quickly to help me . . .
I am poor and needy;
   may the Lord think of me.
You are my help and my deliverer;
   O my God, do not delay.[6]

As I wrote about the pits in my past, I remembered so clearly what it felt like to lash out in anger, to be swallowed whole by red-hot rage. I remembered the feeling that bitterness produced in me—the very real feeling of my heart being squeezed too tightly, of scarcely being able to breathe too deeply.

And as I remembered those feelings, I compared them to the feelings of today—of whatever my "normal" life looks like at this present moment. I see how vastly different they are.

Oh, I'm so glad! I'm thankful to be free—to find myself in the pleasant place he's led me. It makes me want to fall on my face in worship, to say "thank you" again and again and again.

How can I not love him when he's rescued me from such misery, such heartache? And when passion is my response, I pray never to forget the place from which he rescued me.

I don't want to forget because pits lie all along the way, and I slip in them as I go through life. But he's rescued me in the past, and he will rescue me again. Yes, I want to avoid pits in the road, but I'm by no means perfect and will fall in again.

Forgiven

When was the last time you read the story of the sinful woman in Luke 7? If it's been awhile, grab your Bible and read it there, or read it below.

Now one of the Pharisees invited Jesus to have dinner

with him, so he went to the Pharisee's house and re-
clined at the table. When a woman who had lived a
sinful life in that town learned that Jesus was eating
at the Pharisee's house, she brought an alabaster jar
of perfume, and as she stood behind him at his feet
weeping, she began to wet his feet with her tears. Then
she wiped them with her hair, kissed them and poured
perfume on them.

When the Pharisee who had invited him saw this,
he said to himself, "If this man were a prophet, he
would know who is touching him and what kind of
woman she is—that she is a sinner."

Jesus answered him, "Simon, I have something to
tell you."

"Tell me, teacher," he said.

"Two men owed money to a certain moneylender.
One owed him five hundred denarii, and the other
fifty. Neither of them had the money to pay him back,
so he canceled the debts of both. Now which of them
will love him more?"

Simon replied, "I suppose the one who had the
bigger debt canceled."

"You have judged correctly," Jesus said.

Then he turned toward the woman and said to
Simon, "Do you see this woman? I came into your
house. You did not give me any water for my feet, but
she wet my feet with her tears and wiped them with
her hair. You did not give me a kiss, but this woman,
from the time I entered, has not stopped kissing my
feet. You did not put oil on my head, but she has
poured perfume on my feet. Therefore, I tell you, her
many sins have been forgiven—for she loved much.
But he who has been forgiven little loves little." (Luke
7:36–47)

Reading this story always makes me feel a little uncomfortable.
I feel like I'm peeking in on something I shouldn't be seeing—
catching someone at a vulnerable moment.

Something feels so private about this woman's display of passion for Jesus. But I remind myself that it wasn't private. It took place in a public setting, with others watching—or trying not to watch, maybe—uncomfortably.

I can relate to Simon's unease with this woman as he wonders at her incredible behavior. For it's not until the end that we learn what in the world is behind her actions. From the beginning, it's only Jesus—omniscient God made man—who knows the whole story.

I want to love passionately like this woman. To have passion that knows no pride, passion that goes where Jesus goes even if it means going someplace I've not been before, passion that is more concerned with the object of my passion than with what others think.

Can you imagine?

This woman—this sinful woman, defined as a prostitute in the notes in my Bible—went to a house occupied by a Pharisee, a religious leader. She went to a house where she knew she'd be rejected, scorned, refused. She went knowing that disapproval and disdain would greet her, but she went anyway—because that's where Jesus was. Jesus, the one who could offer complete and lasting forgiveness for her sins. Jesus, God incarnate, who would have mercy according to his great compassion, blot out her transgressions, wash away her iniquity, and cleanse her from her sin (see Ps. 51:1–2).

Jesus, the fulfillment of the law, is the only one who could make it possible for the words of Isaiah 1:18 to be true for her, "Though your sins are like scarlet, they shall be as white as snow; though they are red as crimson, they shall be like wool." Jesus, the only one who could take a scarlet woman and make her pure enough to be his bride.

That's what explains her passion.

The one who has been forgiven much loves much.

I've been tempted to think that I haven't been forgiven all that much. I grew up in a Christian family, as a small child asked Jesus into my heart, and I can't remember a time when I've not known God. I don't have a dramatic testimony of living a sinful life and meeting Jesus and turning it all around. No drugs, no sex, no alcohol. As a high school student, I remember feeling like I had a boring testimony.

But I'm reminded of the truth Paul taught: "There is no difference, for all have sinned and fall short of the glory of God" (Rom. 3:22–23). It doesn't matter if my testimony keeps people on the edge of their seats as they wait for the dramatic moment of conversion. *There is no difference.* Sin is sin is sin. And I have been forgiven.

As I long for the kind of passion I see in this sinful woman, I realize that what will bring it about in part is my awareness of how much I've been forgiven. I need to take to heart that it is my sin—whatever form it takes—that put Jesus on the cross to die and pay the price of my salvation. "Without the shedding of blood there is no forgiveness," wrote the author of Hebrews (9:22). My sin required the blood of Jesus for forgiveness.

The other morning as I met with God, I asked him to teach me more about how much I've been forgiven. I realized that the majority of what I've needed forgiveness for has been sins I've committed in the midst of walking with him. I don't remember lots of dramatic sin in my life before becoming a Christian at the age of four or five, but I can remember lots of sin in my life *after* becoming a Christian.

To think of the sin in my heart—the hateful attitudes, the arrogant pride, the willful disobedience—that I've committed as a believer—as one who loves God and has promised to "trust and obey" him alone—breaks my heart. I see the ways in which I've not acted as the new creation he's made me in Christ, and I imagine it disappoints the Father and breaks his heart as well.

I have been forgiven much. May it cause me to love him more and more.

Such awareness is not to wallow in guilt or self-pity or to compare my sins with the sins of others. Rather, such awareness is to make me love him more. So I pray that God will make me aware of my sin, prompt me to seek forgiveness, and to respond to such forgiveness with love.

Becoming the Beloved

Like "Thy will be done," a prayer for a greater desire for God will always be answered with a resounding "Yes!" The story of Scripture is the story of God pursuing relationship with us, his passionate love for us. He has gone to great lengths to show how much he loves us, and wants us to love him passionately in return. We find that passion as we discover who we really are.

As Brennan Manning has written, "The recovery of passion begins with the recovery of my true self as the beloved."[7] He goes on to write about the apostle John: "If John were to be asked, 'What is your primary identity, your most coherent sense of yourself?' he would not reply, 'I am a disciple, an apostle, an evangelist,' but 'I am the one Jesus loves.'"[8] How would you answer the question?

When I did Beth Moore's study *Believing God* a few years ago, I memorized what she calls "The Shield of Faith."[9] It goes like this: God is who he says he is. God can do what he says he can do. I am who God says I am. I can do all things through Christ. God's Word is alive and active in me.

I am who God says I am. You are who God says you are. We are who he, as the Creator, says we are. It is *his* opinion that matters.

Who does he say we are? It takes only a flip through the Bible to see:

- We are his people, the sheep of his pasture.
- We are the apple of his eye.
- We are his beloved.
- We are the body of Christ.
- We are the redeemed.
- We are loved.
- We are his passion.

Believing who he says we are is vital to passion.

A Consuming Fire

Burning passion. The phrase just sounds right, doesn't it?

One of the names for God found in Scripture is *Esh Oklah*, or Consuming Fire. "For the LORD your God is a consuming fire," Moses told the people of Israel as they stood ready to enter the Promised Land (Deut. 4:24).

Moses knew something about the fire of God. The story of the burning bush was taught to me in Sunday school as the teacher moved figures around on the flannel graph to illustrate. Since I don't have a flannel graph set, you'll have to use your imagination to picture the scene from Exodus 3:1–6:

Now Moses was tending the flock of Jethro his father-in-law, the priest of Midian, and he led the flock to the far side of the desert and came to Horeb, the mountain of God. There the angel of the LORD appeared to him in flames of fire from within a bush. Moses saw that though the bush was on fire it did not burn up. So Moses thought, "I will go over and see this strange sight—why the bush does not burn up."

When the LORD saw that he had gone over to look, God called to him from within the bush, "Moses! Moses!"

And Moses said, "Here I am."

"Do not come any closer," God said. "Take off your sandals, for the place where you are standing is holy ground." Then he said, "I am the God of your father, the God of Abraham, the God of Isaac and the God of Jacob." At this, Moses hid his face, because he was afraid to look at God.

God's passion is a burning passion. In reading this story and thinking about God's passion, I'm struck anew that the bush didn't burn up. God's passion isn't a fire that destroys. His consuming fire is a refiner's fire (see Mal. 3:2), one that burns away impurity, leaving us aflame with passion, but not turned to ash.

I want to burn with passion for God. I want God to fan the flame of my desire for him, to burn away all that is impure in me, to be a fire fed with his Word.

But such a desire for passion requires trust. Do I trust him to burn the impurity in me without burning me? Do I trust him to set me ablaze with passion without turning me to ash?

The Lesson from Camp

As I've prayed for passion, God has answered. In fact, he answered with a lesson I'll never forget. I blogged about it just after it happened:

I don't sleep well at [Girl Scout] camp. I usually lay awake for hours each night, and often get panicky when I can't fall asleep. The result is that I pray like mad for each girl and her family, hoping that'll send me off to sleep. *Maybe that's why I can't sleep at camp*, I thought. *It's so I will pray*. But this weekend, I prayed for each girl and her family *before* leaving for camp, hoping that I'd then be able to sleep.

So I went to bed on Friday night, tired and hoping to fall asleep quickly. It didn't happen. I listened to my iPod for more than an hour (I downloaded *Greatest Hymns* by Selah from iTunes before I left—if you're looking for a new hymns CD, go get this one!) and was so tired, but couldn't sleep.

As I lay there, tired and thirsty and longing for morning with everything in me, wishing so hard to be home, I remembered something my friend Cheryl said she'd pray for—for God to have something specifically for me at camp.

I've been thinking a lot about passion lately— about what passion for God really looks like, what it *feels* like. I read the psalms each day and want to long for God the way the psalmists do. I pray for such passion. Another thing I pray for each day is for God *himself* to teach me. I love learning from great teachers, and always will. But I want God to teach me himself, too.

In the dark and quiet of a sleepless night, these verses came to my mind:

> As the deer pants for streams of water,
>   so my soul pants for you, O God.
> My soul thirsts for God, for the living God.
>   When can I go and meet with God?
> Psalm 42:1–2

> My soul waits for the Lord
>   more than watchmen wait for the morning,
>   more than watchmen wait for the morning.
> Psalm 130:6

For the first time, I felt like I really experienced what those verses are talking about. Incredible thirst that I couldn't ignore. And a desperation for morning. Yearning for dawn with every fiber of my being.

When I got up the next morning (after an hour or two of sleep—finally), I realized that as awful and horrible as the night was, it was also a gift. *Because God taught me what I'd been asking for.* He showed me first-hand what those psalms describe. He showed me that kind of thirst, that kind of eager waiting for morning. And he taught it to me in a way I'll never forget.[10]

Pray for passion—and watch for God to answer.

Passionate People

In addition to prayer, I've found that community is essential to developing passion for God. My closest friends share a similar desire to develop a greater awareness of God's presence in daily life. We talk about the ways in which we see God act, pray for one another, and rejoice together when those prayers are answered.

My Bible study group is yet another community. We come together to gain knowledge of God and Scripture, and that gives me a greater appetite for God as we learn and grow in "knowledge and depth of insight" (Phil. 1:9).

Godly teachers help me develop passion for God. From Bible study to church to older women who can mentor me—they enhance my desire to follow God more closely.

In short, being around passionate people makes me passionate, too!

I think that's why the writer of Hebrews encourages us so strongly to meet with other believers. Hebrews 10:25 says, "Let us not give up meeting together, as some are in the habit of doing, but let us encourage one another—and all the more as you see the Day approaching."

We find passion with other believers. If passion is something we want, we need to be where other believers are.

R.S.V.P.

What moves you to passion? Music, poetry, story? Are those things part of your quiet time? What do you love about God? Tell him!

In pursuing passion, the best tool I've found is the book of Psalms. David and the other psalmists express such passion and desire for God that I'm always moved to want what they have.

Read through the psalms and make them personal, turning them into prayers to God. Many of them are already suited to prayer—just pray them out loud straight from Scripture. Others may require a little tweaking, as you change words like *you* and *your* to *me* and *my*.

For example, Psalm 103:2–6 would look like this:

> Praise the Lord, O my soul, and forget not all his
> benefits—
> You have forgiven me all my sins and healed all my
> diseases,
> You redeemed my life from the pit and crowned me
> with love and compassion,
> You satisfy my desires with good things so that my
> youth is renewed like the eagle's.
> You work righteousness and justice for me.

It's possible to read and pray through the Psalms in a month by reading five psalms a day. Here's how: on day one, read Psalms 1, 31, 61, 91, and 121. On day two, read Psalms 2, 32, 62, 92, 122. By the time you get to day thirty, you'll read Psalm 30, Psalm 60, Psalm 90, Psalm 120, and Psalm 150. This works great—just be sure to have some extra time on day twenty-nine when it's time to read Psalm 119!

Pray for passion. Ask God to set your heart on fire with love and passion for him. Ask him to make you thrill to hear and read his Word. Pursue him and ask him to reveal himself to you each day.

These are all things that God wants for you. If you desire them, he'll be only too glad to give them to you.

Finally, are you spending time with passionate people? Are you regularly meeting with other believers, or have you given up the habit? Get plugged back in! What do you need to do to make that happen?

Do you have friends who pursue passion for God? How can you meet together and encourage one another "all the more as you see the Day approaching"?

It's Time to Respond

So, the invitation is there. God wants to meet with you—each day. He wants to bless you—with his Word, his Spirit, his power. He knows exactly what each day holds for you and has all you need to live it for his glory.

"Come away with me," he beckons.

Rest, satisfaction, intimacy, energy—he has it for you in abundance. Wisdom and understanding—he himself will teach you.

So how will you respond?

We could assume that because we're the ones receiving the invitation, our response is without effort. But I'm not sure that's true. The one doing the inviting has the lion's share of work, for sure. But whenever we receive an invitation, we have some responsibility, and have to give some effort to it.

How will we respond to the invitation? What will we have to say *no* to in order to accept it? What must we do to prepare, to be ready? A wedding, a birthday party, dinner at a friend's home—all require some effort on our part to accept.

The joy of anticipation—looking forward to what's coming—makes the effort worth it on our part. We don't mind saying *no* to something in order to attend a friend's wedding. We're glad to bring a gift, to dress for the occasion. To make arrangements and travel plans for the joy set before us.

The invitation has been sent. God invites you to get away with him each day. How will you respond? What arrangements do you need to make?

Will you respond at all? Or will you decide at the last minute, without a thought to the host? It's definitely your choice.

R.S.V.P. means this: *Repondez, s'il vous plaît.* Respond please.

I love old books. And old books on etiquette and manners are ones I love to find and collect. It's fun to read about manners of dress from years ago, or the proper way to help a lady down from a carriage.

One of the books I've found is *Our Manners at Home and Abroad: A Complete Manual on the Manners, Customs, and Social Forms of the Best American Society Including Specimen Letters, Invitations, Acceptances and Regrets Compiled from the Leading and Most Reliable Modern Authorities.* How's that for a title? Published in Denver by D. D. Darrow and Company in 1884, it's full of all kinds of delightful tidbits—"Rich Versus Showy Dress," "Masquerades and Fancy-Dress Theatricals," "Indiscriminate Correspondence," and "Requisites to a Successful Dinner-Party."

Some of the information is not really applicable for today— can't remember the last time I dismounted from a carriage. But it's surprising how little good manners have changed.

In regard to accepting invitations, here's what the book says: "An invitation should be answered with promptness. . . . It is rude to decline an invitation without expressing regret, and a refusal should never be sent without giving an explanation."

When it comes right down to it, good manners are timeless.

When the God of all creation invites, we'd do well to respond. The choice is up to you. Will you take him up on his invitation?

I pray that you will. For it is one of the most important invitations you'll ever receive. I hope you'll respond *yes*—that you'll take him up on all he's offering to you. It will change your life.

So we end as we began—with God's invitation to you:

My Child,
Come away with me by yourself
and get some rest.
Be still and know that I am God.

It's Time to Respond

I will satisfy you with good things
and restore your strength.
I will waken you morning by morning
and I myself will teach you;
I will direct you in the way you should go.
My compassion never fails;
great is my faithfulness.
Wait for me.
Put your hope in me
and you will not be disappointed.
You are mine and I love you,
Your Abba

How will you respond?

Resources

These resources have been of particular help to me in my journey of quiet time. If you have others you love, I'd love to hear about them and add them to my library, too. Visit my blog at http://www.thesimplewife.typepad.com.

Books

Benson, Robert. *Living Prayer*. New York: Jeremy P. Tarcher/Putnam, 1998.

This is one of my favorite books on prayer—and one of my favorite books in general. I have read it many times and always find something new with each reading. If you're looking for a book to help shape your view of prayer and to help you view prayer as a way of life, this is it.

————. *Venite: A Book of Daily Prayer*. New York: Jeremy P. Tarcher/Putnam, 2000.

This is the prayer book that I use each morning. Based upon the *Book of Common Prayer*, it includes different offices to be said throughout the day, and each includes songs from Scripture and readings from the Psalms and Gospels. I love the structure it offers, as well as the practice of reading through the Psalms and the words of Jesus every month.

Buchanan, Mark. *The Holy Wild: Trusting in the Character of God.* Sisters, OR: Multnomah, 2003.

In this book, Mark Buchanan examines the character of God, opening our eyes to the multifaceted aspects of his personality. If your view of God has grown routine, this book will open your eyes and your heart to loving God Most High.

————. *The Rest of God: Restoring Your Soul by Restoring Sabbath.* Nashville: Nelson, 2006.

Rest is a gift that many people do not receive. If you're interested in the idea of rest, learning how to keep the Sabbath, or knowing how to be still with God, this is a must read. Each chapter also includes a Sabbath liturgy—a practical step in learning to rest.

Fee, Gordon D., and Douglas Stuart. *How to Read the Bible for All Its Worth.* Grand Rapids: Zondervan, 2003.

This book is an excellent tool for anyone wanting to study the Word. A little bit like a textbook, this volume clearly explains the different genres found in Scripture (epistle, narrative, gospel, parable, prophecy, psalms, wisdom, law, and revelation) and how best to approach and study them. See also Mears, *What the Bible Is All About.*

Fleming, Jean. *Feeding Your Soul: A Quiet Time Handbook.* Colorado Springs, CO: NavPress, 1999.

This book is a quiet time handbook, filled with all kinds of helpful tools and practical information on the "how" of having a quiet time. It includes exercises to teach you study techniques and questions for discussion and reflection.

Johnson, Jan. *Enjoying the Presence of God.* Colorado Springs, CO: NavPress, 1996.

Inspired by *The Practice of the Presence of God* by Brother Lawrence, Jan wrote this book to give readers practical insights into how to practice God's presence as they go about their ordinary lives. She shows that practicing God's presence can turn your ordinary day into something extraordinary.

Lawrence, Brother. *The Practice of the Presence of God*. Boston: New Seeds Books, 2005.

In this small volume, Brother Lawrence shares his practice of dwelling with God in each moment of each day—whether at work in the kitchen or at prayer in the chapel. He offers wise counsel for doing everything to God's glory and for turning your thoughts constantly to God in the midst of whatever task you undertake—turning all secular things to a sacred practice.

Lee-Thorp, Karen. *The Story of Stories: The Bible in Narrative Form*. Colorado Springs, CO: NavPress, 1995.

Written in an easy-to-understand and engaging style, this book will walk you through Scripture—from Genesis to Revelation, giving you a broad view of the Bible as a story of God's redemptive love for his people. This guide will give you the big picture of Scripture to see how it all fits together as a whole.

Manning, Brennan. *Abba's Child*. Colorado Springs, CO: NavPress, 1994.

Part of finding passion for God is knowing he is passionate for us. The back cover of this book summarizes its message well: "The liberating message of this book is that God longs for us to know in the depths of our being that he loves and accepts us as we are. God is our 'Abba,' our loving Father, who knows us far better than we know ourselves . . . , loves us far more than we can imagine, and longs to bring us into deeper, more joyful, passionate fellowship with himself."

Mears, Henrietta C. *What the Bible Is All About*. Ventura, CA: Regal, 1997.

This book is about exactly what the title says. It begins with some basic Bible information, then moves right into book-by-book summary and teaching. Each chapter also includes a reading plan to read through that particular book of the Bible in a week. If you're ready to dig in and study the Word, this is a great tool to use.

Spangler, Ann. *Praying the Names of God*. Grand Rapids, MI: Zondervan, 2004.

In this book, Ann Spangler teaches readers to pray the various names of God found in Scripture. She teaches the meaning of each name, highlighting each one in terms of God's character and our response to him. As you learn the different names of our heavenly Father, you'll learn more about him and be moved to pray in new ways.

Wald, Oletta. *The Joy of Discovery in Bible Study*. Minneapolis: Augsburg, 1975.

This is the book that taught me how to study the Bible on my own, using the inductive Bible study method. A great resource for Bible study during your quiet time, this small book will open your eyes to see that you can study Scripture on your own.

Wangerin, Walter, Jr. *Reliving the Passion*. Grand Rapids, MI: Zondervan, 1992.

Based on the gospel of Mark, this book is a guided reading through the season of Lent. As you journey with Jesus toward Calvary and experience the anticipation and grief of the cross, you will discover new joy in the resurrection.

Online Resources

Blueletterbible.org

I use this Web site almost every day as I study the Bible. It allows you to search Scripture by topic, reference, or keyword and includes many translations for comparison and study. It also includes easy-to-use Greek and Hebrew lexicons, maps, charts, and more.

Cyberhymnal.org

I love singing hymns and hearing the rich treasure of theology so many of them teach. This Web site includes everything you could ever want to know about hymns—search by tune, by title, by topic, by Scripture. You can listen to the hymns right on the site, and see all the lyrics (even verse three—the one that never seems to get sung at church!). Most hymns also include information about the author and the story behind that particular hymn.

Notes

Introduction: Have You Misplaced God?

1. Beth Moore, "Living Proof Live" (Phoenix, AZ, December 1–2, 2006).
2. Jan Johnson, *Enjoying the Presence of God* (Colorado Springs, CO, 1996), 11.
3. Rueben P. Job and Norman Shawchuck, *A Guide to Prayer for All God's People* (Nashville: Upper Room Books, 1990), 11.
4. Maud Hart Lovelace, *Betsy Was a Junior* (New York: HarperTrophy, 1979), 166.

Chapter 1: Finding God

Epigraph. Robert Benson, *Venite: A Book of Daily Prayer* (New York: Jeremy P. Tarcher/Putnam, 2000), 11.
1. This verse taken from ibid., 156.
2. G. I. Williamson, *The Westminster Confession of Faith for Study Classes* (Philadelphia: Presbyterian and Reformed, 1964), 24.
3. Beth Moore, introductory session video to *Living Beyond Yourself* (Nashville: LifeWay Church Resources, 1998), 8.

Chapter 2: Finding a Purpose

Epigraph. Benson, Psalm 103, in *Venite*, 166.

1. Brennan Manning, *Abba's Child* (Colorado Springs, CO: NavPress, 1994), 51.
2. Can you relate? If you're ready to pursue a simpler life, check out my book *Living Simply: Choosing Less in a World of More* (Sisters, OR: Multnomah Books, 2006).
3. Moore, "Living Proof Live."
4. Ann Spangler, *Praying the Names of God* (Grand Rapids, MI: Zondervan, 2004), 130.
5. Joseph Addison, as quoted in *And I Quote*, comp. Ashton Applewhite, William R. Evans III, and Andrew Frothingham (New York: St. Martin's, 1992), 137.
6. http://notthatgirlthisgirl.blogspot.com/2007/10/its-all-good.html.
7. Susan Smith, from a personal e-mail dated December 27, 2007.
8. Manning, *Abba's Child*, 126–28.
9. "The Wedding Banquet" by Miriam Therese Winter.
10. Benson, *Venite*, 200–201.

Chapter 3: Finding a Place

Epigraph. "Give Me Jesus." American spiritual.
1. C. S. Lewis, *Prince Caspian* (New York: Collier Books, 1970), 137.
2. Ibid., 138.
3. YouthFront. For more information, visit their Web site at www .youthfront.com.
4. Brother Lawrence, *The Practice of the Presence of God* (Boston: New Seeds Books, 2005), vii.
5. Jennifer from Redlands, CA. E-mail. Used by permission.
6. These verses were taken from Benson, *Venite*. They have been paraphrased in order to speak them to God as prayer.
7. See http://livingproofministries.blogspot.com/2007/09/90-days-with-one-and-only_17.html.

Chapter 4: Finding a Practice

Epigraph. Henrietta C. Mears, *What the Bible Is All About* (Ventura, CA: Regal, 1997), 21.
1. For all the lyrics to "Amazing Grace," visit http://www.cyberhymnal .org/htm/a/m/a/amazing_grace.htm.
2. Dictionary.com Unabridged (v 1.1), s.v. "secure." Based on the *Random House Unabridged Dictionary* (New York: Random House, 2006).
3. Ibid.

4. Mears, *What the Bible Is All About*, 21.

5. Ibid., 24–25.

Chapter 5: Finding Prayer

Epigraph. Joseph Scriven, "What a Friend We Have in Jesus." For all the lyrics to this hymn, visit http://cyberhymnal.org/htm/w/a/f/wafwhij.htm.

1. Ann Spangler, *Praying the Names of God* (Grand Rapids: Zondervan, 2004).

2. Benson, "Day 21, Psalter: Evening," in *Venite*, 169.

3. C. S. Lewis, *The Voyage of the Dawn Treader* (New York: Macmillan Publishing Company, 1970), 174.

4. Beth Moore, Women of Faith preconference (Denver, CO, September 21, 2007).

5. Joanne Heim, *Living Simply: Choosing Less in a World of More* (Sisters, OR: Multnomah Books, 2006), 204.

6. See http://livingproofministries.blogspot.com/2007/09/dial-up-from-forest.html.

7. Beth Moore, session 1 video to *Living Beyond Yourself* (Nashville: LifeWay Church Resources, 1998), 30.

Chapter 6: Finding Perseverance

1. Dictionary.com Unabridged (v 1.1), s.v. "perseverance." Based on the *Random House Unabridged Dictionary* (New York: Random House, 2006).

2. Ibid.

3. Beth Moore, Women of Faith preconference (Denver, CO, September 21, 2007).

4. Beth Moore, *Jesus the One and Only* (Nashville: LifeWay Church Resources, 2000), 97.

5. Job and Shawchuck, *Guide to Prayer*, 16.

6. John Wesley, letter to Mr. John Trembath, August 17, 1760, in *The Works of the Reverend John Wesley, A. M.*, by John Emory, vol. 6 (New York: Mason and Lane, 1839), 750.

Chapter 7: Finding Passion

Epigraph. Benson, *Venite*, 7.

1. *Webster's Ninth New Collegiate Dictionary* (Springfield, MA: Merriam-Webster, 1987), s.v. "passion."

2. Ibid.
3. Walter Wangerin Jr., *Reliving the Passion* (Grand Rapids, MI: Zondervan, 1992), 11.
4. Moore, *Jesus the One and Only*, 151.
5. Bill Thrall, Bruce McNicol, and John Lynch, *TruFaced* (Colorado Springs, CO: NavPress, 2003).
6. See http://thesimplewife.typepad.com/the_simple_wife/2007/10/the-big-pit-in-.html.
7. Manning, *Abba's Child*, 125.
8. Ibid., 126.
9. Beth Moore, "The Shield of Faith," in *Believing God* (Nashville: Broadman & Holman, 2004).
10. See http://thesimplewife.typepad.com/the_simple_wife/2007/11/the-lesson-from.html.

About the Author

Joanne Heim is the author of *Living Simply: Choosing Less in a World of More* and the coauthor (with her husband, Toben) of *Happily Ever After: A Real-Life Look at Your First Year of Marriage and Beyond* and *What's Your Story? An Interactive Guide to Building Community*. She is also a contributor to *Daily Seeds: From Women Who Walk in Faith*, a devotional for women from Moody's *Midday Connection*, and has written or ghostwritten a number of Bible studies and study guides.

Joanne has been a guest on numerous radio programs, including *Focus on the Family*, Moody's *Midday Connection*, and *HomeWord* with Jim Burns. She has also appeared on television, including LeSea Broadcasting's program *The Harvest Show*. She has written for and been featured in various publications, including *Focus on the Family*, *Bridal Guide*, *Everyday Woman*, and *Marriage* (formerly *Marriage Encounter*). Previously Joanne worked in the publishing industry as a publicist, copywriter, and editor.

Joanne and Toben were married in 1991, and both graduated from Whitworth College in Spokane, Washington, in 1993. She has degrees in communication studies and French, and is presently working toward a master's degree in biblical studies at Denver Seminary.

Joanne is mom to Audrey and Emma. She writes in between Girl Scout meetings, volunteering at school, and being crafty. The Heim family lives in Denver.

You can read more from Joanne each day on her blog: http://www.thesimplewife.typepad.com.

Also by Joanne Heim

The proposal . . . the planning . . . the wedding . . . the honeymoon . . . then what? Many people think they will become better versions of themselves once they are married, but there are other expectations to deal with too—finances, sex, disagreements, spirituality, household chores, and in-laws.

Written with openness and brimming with practical advice, Toben and Joanne Heim will help you establish realistic expectations and goals for your marriage and find happily ever after.

ISBN: 978-0-8254-2758-9